UNFAITHFUL
ANGELS

UNFAITHFUL ANGELS

HOW SOCIAL WORK HAS
ABANDONED ITS MISSION

Harry Specht

Mark E. Courtney

THE FREE PRESS

The Free Press
A Division of Simon & Schuster Inc.
1230 Avenue of the Americas
New York, N.Y. 10020

First Free Press Paperback Edition 1995

Printed in the United States of America

printing number

8   9   10

Library of Congress Cataloging-in-Publication Data

Specht, Harry.
   Unfaithful angels: how social work has abandoned its mission/ Harry Specht and Mark E. Courtney.
    p. cm.
  ISBN 0–02–874086–6
  1. Social service—United States. 2. Psychotherapy—Social aspects—United States.—3. Social workers—United States.
4. Psychotherapists—United States.—I. Courtney, Mark E.
II. Title.
HV91.S6292 1994
361.973—dc20   93–23934
                                                      CIP

The authors acknowledge, with thanks, permission to take material from the following papers: Mark Courtney, "Psychiatric Social Workers and the Early Days of Private Practice," *Social Service Review* 66:2 (June 1992); Harry Specht, "Social Work and the Popular Psychotherapies," *Social Service Review* 64:3 (September 1990).

To the pioneers

Jane Addams and Mary Richmond

Those sweetly smiling angels with pensive looks, innocent faces, and cash-boxes for hearts

—Honoré de Balzac, *Cousin Bette*, 1846

For we must consider that we shall be a City upon a hill. The eyes of all people are upon us, so that if we shall deal falsely with our God in this work we have undertaken, and so cause Him to withdraw His present help from us, we shall be made a story and a byword to the world.

—John Winthrop, "A Model of Christian Charity," a sermon delivered on board the Arabella, 1630

CONTENTS

———•◦•———

PREFACE

———— •‥‥• ————

I have been actively engaged in social work for close to 50 years, a span that holds almost half the history of the profession in the United States. In those years social work has changed continuously in response to changes in American society. For example, in the 1930s there was an abatement of the previous decade's "psychiatric deluge," as social workers turned from studying Freud to attend to the social devastation brought about by the Great Depression. The radicalism of the 1930s gave way in the subsequent decade to a patriotic fervor supporting total mobilization of resources to fight World War II. During the McCarthy era of the 1950s the profession reacted in much the same way as other parts of society: generally, social work became more conservative. This was manifest in a preoccupation with professionalization, the refinement of clinical techniques, and the use of more sophisticated analytic methods.

Nor were social workers found wanting in the civil rights and anti-war movements of the 1960s and 1970s. "We're relevant too!" said many members of the profession. Community organization, advocacy, and anti-poverty programs became the order of the day. Overwhelmed, the psychiatric social workers who had reigned professionally supreme for many years beat an ignominious retreat; however, though down, they were not out. In the later 1970s they reappeared with a new name, clinical social work, to ride the crest of a new social work wave: now social workers went into private practice in droves—to do psychotherapy. They were doing all shades and varieties of psychotherapy, and they were doing it with a new clientele.

When I first came to know social workers half a century ago, they had a mission that was, to me, appealing and significant: to

help poor people, to improve community life, and to solve difficult social problems. But times have changed. Today, a significant proportion of social workers are practicing psychotherapy,
and doing so privately, with a primarily middle-class, professional, Caucasian clientele in the 20- to 40-year age group. The
poor have not gone away; there are more of them than at any
time in recent memory. Community life has deteriorated, and
our social problems have gotten more difficult and complex. Certainly many professional social workers are still committed to the
public social services, to helping poor people, and dealing with
social problems like homelessness and child neglect, but a large
part of the profession is adrift in the psychotherapeutic seas.

Many young people continue to be drawn to our profession by
their passion for social justice and a desire to help those who are
in most need, such as AIDS victims and the frail aged. These are
the kinds of practitioners and students the profession needs if it
is to realize its original mission. Increasingly, though, it becomes
more difficult to sustain and nourish a passion for and commitment to that kind of mission because the thinking of too many
social workers—like the thinking of too many other Americans—
is dominated by a psychotherapeutic ethos. It is our intention in
this book to stir debate about social work's purpose in American
life and, it is hoped, to persuade Americans to chart a new course
for social work—to give the profession a 21st-century means of
realizing its significant social mission.

Mark Courtney came to this project via a route different from
mine. During the course of his training as a clinical psychologist,
he worked with abused and neglected children in residential
care—a traditional social work concern. While he found his clinical skills of some use in helping these youths, he became increasingly aware of the wide range of social problems they and their
families faced which were not amenable to psychotherapeutic intervention. It seemed to him that a broader focus was called for.
Eventually he came to believe that social work was a place where
he could articulate and refine his developing ideas about family
and children's services. When he began to study the current
scene in social work in more depth, however, he found that his
vision of social work's raison d'être appeared to be shared by
fewer and fewer social workers. In fact, it seemed that most of his

new colleagues had more in common with his old colleagues—psychotherapists—than they did with his ideal social worker. My growing concern over the state of the profession to which I have dedicated myself, together with Mark's realization that he has joined the profession at a time when the "social" in social work may be rendered meaningless, led to our collaboration on this book.

A number of people provided us with support and counsel as we developed our ideas. Because I am Mark Courtney's senior by many years, I have many more people to thank than he. Some of my good friends who have been especially encouraging are Neil and Barbara Gilbert, Carol and Berkeley Johnson, and Ed and Harriet Nathan. Neil Gilbert, Ed Nathan, Henry Miller, and Robert Specht, my brother, read the manuscript and gave many helpful suggestions. Other colleagues who advised us on various issues are William Smelser, Bart Grossman, and William McKinley Runyan. Needless to say, not all of the people mentioned agree with us, and none are responsible for what is written here.

I am deeply indebted to my secretary, Kathryn Vergeer, who has been supremely patient about producing numerous drafts of the manuscript. She also contributed comments on the content and set us straight on some refined points of grammar. Jim Steele and Paul Terrell, my colleagues at Berkeley, have given me a great deal of help in getting my dean-work done so I could pay attention to some of these issues.

I owe thanks to several schools who gave me a congenial place to work when I could get away from Berkeley: Columbia University School of Social Work; Hunter College School of Social Work; the Department of Social Administration at the London School of Economics, the National Institute for Social Work in London, the New Mexico Highlands University School of Social Work, and Institut d'Études Sociales in Geneva. My first opportunities to present some of these ideas were provided by the School of Social Work at California State University, Fresno, and Region C, California Chapter of the National Association of Social Workers.

In addition to the colleagues mentioned above who were kind

enough to read various drafts of the book, Mark thanks his wife, Camille Farrington. She deserves much credit for her unending and multifaceted support of this undertaking and her close critical reading of early drafts of the manuscript. And I owe much to my wife, Riva, for many years of love, support, and assistance.

Harry Specht

CHAPTER ONE

SOCIAL WORK AND PSYCHOTHERAPY IN THE AMERICAN COMMUNITY

———— ••••• ————

Let us begin this book with a game called "Find the faith healer— find the social worker—find the psychotherapist." Here are seven brief portraits of helping professionals. See if you can pick out which is which.

Carol Newhouse does psychic reading of past lives. She writes that this is helpful with "insights into relationship entanglements, life purpose, job creativity, addictive behavior, psychic/spiritual growth." She works from "her experience with women's spirituality/ goddess religion spirit-channeling/trance-dancing, Buddhist/Taoist philosophy and meditation, and Native American astrology."[1]

At a recent conference Frances Brown, Alexandra Nathanson, and Charlotte Riley gave a workshop, "Narcissistic Impairment in Men Clients Treated by Women Therapists: A Study of Transference, Countertransference, and Cultural Reality." Following is their summary of the workshop content: "Narcissistic disturbance presents special challenges to the female therapist in her work with male clients. In this session, the transference-countertransference dialogue in this treatment situation will be examined."[2]

Cecile Marie writes: "I work with people who need to reacquaint themselves with and polish their own tools, listen more carefully to the dialogue within, separate fact from fiction and synthesize the dissonance. This process is what I call unfolding your wings."[3]

Patricia Bland holds sessions on "Awakening: Rosen Method Body Work." She describes this as follows: "The Sleeping State:

1

When we hold back feelings, we simultaneously tighten muscles. Continued long enough, the holding becomes automatic. A part of us falls asleep and our capacity for emotional and creative expression diminishes.

"The Awaken Process: When I touch the sleeping muscles, gently and deeply, with patience, they begin to awaken. Your body and breath subtly change, and my hands and my words respond."[4]

At another conference, Jean Sanville gave the keynote address: "Theories, Therapies, Therapists: Their Transformations." She spoke of "the intricacies in understanding the patient from a developmental point of view." She views the analyst/patient interchange as "a kind of 'play' which facilitates the patient's development."[5]

Joyce M. Lavey teaches "Making Money Doing What You Love." She writes that "your Higher Self knows your purpose in the universe and how to create work you truly love. Empower yourself by combining your talents and skills with dynamic techniques which unleash your creativity and stimulate your intuition."[6]

Roberta Godbe tells potential clients that "together, we will explore deep levels of being, restructuring subconscious patterns and releasing emotional pain at a cellular level. This type of work involves an honest commitment to transformation which moves beyond mere personal change." Her approach, she says, incorporates "powerful transformational tools to assist in this process including conscious breathwork, hypnotherapy, past life regressions, process work, subtle energy technology, and the healing of conception, birth and prenatal trauma."[7]

Difficult to sort out? Not at all. Although some of these people appear to be faith healers and psychotherapists, all are social workers. They have their master's degrees from schools of social work (M.S.W.) and most of them are licensed to practice clinical social work (L.C.S.W.).[8] All of them are in private practice.

Many readers probably think that social workers are professionals who help poor people and deal with problems of homelessness, child abuse and neglect, and care of the mentally ill and the frail aged. There are many social workers who do work with these kinds of problems. The following are examples:

Mary Longwood is a social worker from a family service agency. She attends a senior recreation center two days a week to help members with their problems. Approximately 250 aged people use the center each day, primarily for the hot midday meal. Mary encourages all members to apply for social and health benefits for which they may be eligible, such as social security or Medicaid. When appropriate, she helps members to get household help so that they can continue to live independently in the community as long as possible. Members sometimes need help in obtaining nursing home care or convalescent hospital care. She frequently meets with the children and grandchildren of these aged people to help their families plan for their care.

Betty Carr is a social worker for a foster care and adoption agency that deals with hard-to-place children. Many of these are older children with emotional problems and children with birth defects, drug addictions, and AIDS. Carr helps potential adoptive parents and foster parents to understand the problems, emotional burdens, and responsibilities they will have in raising these children. Once the children are placed, she continues to oversee the placement and to advise and support the parents.[9]

What makes these social workers different from the first ones we mentioned is that their concern is enabling people to make use of social and community resources: their families, voluntary associations, public services, friends, and so forth. In contrast, psychotherapists are concerned primarily with helping patients deal with problems that are intimately related to their selves. The psychotherapist helps the patient to increase self-esteem—to have higher regard for the self and to care for and protect the self in dealings with other people.

This book tells the story of social work and the psychotherapies, two significant professions that have emerged in the twentieth century. It is not our intention to inform people about how to do either social work or psychotherapy. Scores of other writers have described one or another kind of social work or psychotherapy, and the world will not be made richer by yet one more book on those subjects. Nor is it our primary intention to knock or champion either social work or psychotherapy. Scores of other volumes recount achievements and failures, and the evils and blessings, of both. Little can be said to change the balance of views in these matters.

Although we are dubious about the efficacy of psychotherapy in general and strongly opposed to its use as the major mode of social work practice, we begin with the assumption that both so-cial work and psychotherapy serve important functions in mod-ern life, although neither is fulfilling these functions very well. We believe that social work has abandoned its mission to help the poor and oppressed and to build communality. Instead, many social workers are devoting their energies and talents to careers in psychotherapy. A significant proportion of social work profes-sionals—about 40 percent—are in private practice, serving mid-dle-class clients.

We begin the argument with discussion of the question: Why should Americans care about what becomes of the profession of social work?

WHO SHOULD CARE?

Why aren't there any newspaper headlines about the possibility of social work's becoming a profession devoted to the private practice of psychotherapy? Why aren't people writing to their congressional representatives about it and complaining to the universities about misuse of funds in social work education? The fact is that very few people care about what social workers do and what happens to social work. They should, but they do not, and that is one of the reasons that so many social workers have headed to private practice.

Americans are fair and generous people, responsive to appeals for charity, especially when they are presented with portraits of individuals in need: newspaper and television stories about a family that needs assistance to tend to their child who has a rare disease, natural disasters, organizations of poor people pulling themselves up by their own bootstraps, and others. These per-sonalized stories of heroism in the face of travail frequently elicit enthusiastic public support, and people willingly contribute funds, especially when they can see positive results quickly. But, paradoxically perhaps, Americans turn away from relentless, enduring, grinding, persistent need. Witness the backlash against the homeless, the stinginess of grants to families with dependent children, and public unwillingness to support programs for chronically dependent populations.

Social workers have been society's unwelcome messengers. They have brought unpleasant news about distasteful needs and problems, and society has treated them accordingly—with ambivalence. On the one hand, there is appreciation and applause for the selfless and altruistic spirit of social work. On the other hand, though, and evidence to the contrary notwithstanding, there is an unrelenting suspicion that the welfare benefits and the services and programs provided by professional social workers place a great and unnecessary expense on taxpayers. There is, too, a muted but persistent worry that all of these benefits and services may encourage indolence and dependency.[10] Thus, support for social work and social welfare services is and always has been unwilling and reluctant.

The story with psychotherapy is different. Americans, ever hopeful of finding the philosopher's stone that will turn their leaden feelings into lilting passions and their gloomy present into golden tomorrows, have always been suckers for new psychological elixirs. From phrenology to spiritualism, from Mesmer to Freud, and from Aimee Simple McPherson to Bridie Murphy and Shirley MacLaine, there has always been a healthy market for theories, serious and half-baked, about how to achieve happiness and peace of mind, and more recently, how to raise self-esteem. Professionals in the personal happiness business are well received and well paid.

Therefore, it is no wonder that social workers—if they are paid badly enough, treated with sufficient ill regard, and given the worst of working conditions—will want to open stalls in the psychotherapeutic marketplace. This option was not available to them earlier in the century, but it is now, and they are flocking to that marketplace in droves.

Few of us are not touched in important ways by social work and psychotherapy. The social work profession's continuing growth of interest in psychotherapy is, in large part, a reflection of the psychotherapy market. A growing proportion of Americans seek and can pay for psychotherapy. It was estimated in 1976 that 26 percent of all Americans had been engaged at some time in some form of psychotherapeutic counseling (compared to only 14 percent in 1957); in that 1976 study it was estimated that an additional 11 percent of Americans perceived of themselves as potentially benefiting from psychotherapeutic counseling (compared to only 9 percent in 1957).[11] These percentages are probably even larger today. The proportion of people who report that they believed they could handle problems by themselves declined from 41 percent in 1957 to 35 percent in 1976. Bernie Zilbergeld, author of *The Shrinking of America*, estimates that the proportion of Americans who consulted a mental health expert more than tripled between 1957 and 1976.[12]

The numbers of people touched by social work and social welfare are large too. In 1990, almost 40 million Americans—approximately 15 percent of the population—received some kind of social security benefit. Another 6 percent received some other kind of federally supported aid.[13] There is no count of the population using social services, but in 1984, approximately $5\frac{1}{3}$ million (20 percent) of people sixty-five years of age and older made use of a community service.[14]

The professional legions involved in providing these various kinds of services and benefits constitute a significant part of the work force. Recent estimates range from a low of 100,000 licensed psychotherapists to as many as 250,000 psychotherapists and counselors in the United States.[15]

In 1986 between 365,000 and 500,000 people were counted in the U.S. Census as being engaged in occupations classified as social work.[16] The aged, physically handicapped, financially dependent, developmentally disabled, mentally ill, chemically addicted, sexually abused, and those who have aged parents, children, and other disabled and dependent relatives in need of care are very likely to turn, at some time, to one or another of these professionals for assistance in dealing with their problems.

Social work and psychotherapy emerged in the United States over the past 150 years, and it is important for Americans to understand their significance and meaning. Moreover, the public ought to understand the functions that social work and psychotherapy perform so that they are able to exercise some choice over the roles these professions will play in community life. Whether there is more or less social work and more or less psychotherapy is a significant question for public discussion, and that question can be answered only if the public understands the functions of social work and psychotherapy in modern society.

Both professions represent the best that the twentieth century has been able to offer as ways of dealing with the confounding and perplexing social and emotional problems of living in an advanced industrial society. Psychotherapy, which has its origins in the early nineteenth century, encompasses a profound belief in the perfectibility of the individual. It involves such ideas as: if we think the right thoughts, learn to control and direct our impulses and desires, come to appreciate the beauty of our inner selves, love wisely, protect our self-interests, and so forth, each of us can achieve our personal emotional paradise. These ideas have a dark side too: that most suffering is a matter of personal responsibility.

Social work, a somewhat younger profession, was founded on a strong belief in the perfectibility of society. It involves such ideas as: with proper social engineering of the environment, provision to all people of adequate nutrition, good housing, sufficient income, knowledge of sexual hygiene, quality education, nurturing parents, stimulating recreation, and so on, we can make of our community, at once, utopia, Shangri-la, and the City Beautiful. Social work's original objective was to enable people to create and use a healthful and nurturing social environment. Social workers believed this to be the means to prevent and cure the great social ills of poverty, alcoholism, mental illness, family breakdown, crime, and corruption.

Neither social work nor psychotherapy has come close to achieving these goals. The poor and homeless are still with us; chemical abuse is epidemic; single-parent families are more prevalent than ever before; and, according to the report from a national study by the National Institute of Mental Health done between 1980 and 1984, mental and emotional disturbance plagues at least 40 percent of the population.[17] Thus, social work and psychotherapy are imperfect, their claims to success are dubious, and they are costly. But they are needed and they are used because there are no substantial alternatives to them.

There probably will be alternatives to social work and psychotherapy developed over the next one hundred years, and we will take a stab at formulating an alternative vision for social work later in this book. But for the moment, social work and psychotherapy are the most promising options available for solving the emotional and social problems of living in a highly unpredictable society.

Finally, it is important to tell the story of social work and psychotherapy now, before social work is consumed on one side by psychotherapy and eroded on its other side by neoconservatism. In increasing numbers, social workers are flocking to psychotherapeutic pastures, hanging out their shingles to advertise themselves as psychotherapists just as quickly as licensing laws will permit. For the most part, professional associations of social workers and schools of social work are active participants in the great transformation of social work from a professional corps concerned with helping people deal with their social problems to a major platoon in the psychotherapeutic armies. At the same time, the Reagan and Bush administrations reduced considerably governmental supports for various social services, such as food stamps, school lunches, and child care. More serious, they undermined whatever fragile beliefs Americans have in the values of communality and the importance of providing quality care and services for people in need.

THE RELUCTANT WELFARE STATE

The transformation of the profession of social work into a phalanx in the psychotherapeutic armies and its erosion for lack of financial support from government may result in a great loss to the American community. Social work emerged as a profession in response to the inability of communities and families to deal with poverty, disease, disability, discrimination, oppression, and loneliness. Over the course of this century, there has been built a great institution of social welfare and social services to deal with these problems. Social security, workmen's compensation, public assistance, social casework, child welfare, and services for the mentally ill, the aged, and the developmentally disabled, along with others, constitute the welfare state of the modern era, a bold conception of social responsibility in modern society. Social workers were among its architects, and they should be implementers of its mission: to develop a community-based system of social care. Without such commitment from social workers, the welfare state will be only a collection of programs, some of them in conflict with one another, without a guiding purpose.

The United States has been characterized as a "reluctant" welfare state because Americans have always felt uncertain about the efficacy of providing communal assistance to people in need. In our land of opportunity, with its expanding horizons and open frontiers, Americans tend to believe that anyone who is willing to work can be self-supporting.

It is conceded that there are some "worthy poor" who cannot care for themselves—the frail aged, the orphaned, and the severely disabled are examples—and help is given to these people, but it is given grudgingly and always under circumstances that make the receipt of assistance as unappealing as possible. Relief recipients are always treated as "less eligible," meaning that even the poor who are deemed worthy must be given less than what is received by the lowest-paid workers or less than they would be eligible for if one considered their need against a moderate and decent standard of living. Otherwise, it is feared, too many of the poor—the worthy and the unworthy—will find going on the dole to be more attractive than working for a living.

The unworthy poor—apparently able-bodied men and women who are unemployed, some of whom are homeless, mentally ill, and addicted to drugs, and some of whom seem to be just plain unwilling to work—leave many Americans with an angry feeling about social work and social welfare. Since the civil rights revolution of the 1960s and the War on Poverty to which it gave birth, Americans have become familiar with social science explanations of these problems: the culture of poverty, racism, alienation and anomie, and economic exploitation. But many people have become inured to and impatient with these ideas, perhaps because none of these theories explains these problems sufficiently and perhaps because the problems appear to be intractable.

The 1960s were a heady and hopeful time in which many white middle-class Americans believed that civil rights could be won and poverty abolished at little personal cost. The future appeared to be bright for both the economy and community relations. The answers, as Bob Dylan sang, were "blowin' in the wind." However, the exhilaration of the New Frontier and the Great Society were blown away by public disgust with a costly and unpopular war in Vietnam, which resulted in Lyndon Johnson's decision not to seek a second term, the Democratic party's mishandling of their 1968 presidential convention in Chicago, the revelations of the Watergate hearings, and President Carter's apparent impotence to deal with terrorists and inflation.

Many white Americans believed that minorities had gotten too much in the 1960s and 1970s: too much welfare, too many privileges, and too many jobs that would have gone to whites if awarded on the basis of merit alone, without affirmative action (racial quotas). The reality is that what minorities did get in the 1960s and 1970s was too many headlines. A strong belief that the minorities were given a great deal was created by the extensive coverage given to the various civil rights movements, both non-violent and violent, and to the struggles over affirmative action and job discrimination that continue today in the courts.

Federal outlays for welfare benefits did indeed rise considerably between 1965 and 1988: from $77.1 billion (11.5 percent of gross national product [GNP]) to $885.8 billion (18.5 percent of GNP).[18] But at the same time, a decade of neoconservative government resulted in a substantial rise in the number of Americans living in poverty: to 32 million people in 1988 (13.1 percent of all Americans) compared to 24 million (11.4 percent) a decade earlier.[19] Moreover, although social security and Medicare payments expanded considerably, keeping pace with inflation, payments for the safety-net programs (public assistance, food stamps, and nutrition programs) eroded considerably. There are now more homeless people than at any other time since the Great Depression, and joblessness is unconscionably high. The reluctant welfare state is more reluctant than ever.

THE AGE OF MEANINGLESSNESS

Mid-century in the United States was called the Age of Anxiety; the winding down to the end of this century can best be referred to as the Age of Meaninglessness. The consumerism of our most privileged young people characterizes our great but transitional attachment to things—primarily new, bright, and shiny things, which upon acquisition quickly lose their attractiveness. The satisfaction in acquiring things is brief: they almost immediately become old, unstylish, and outmoded.

We are saturated with sensation by the media, primarily television, which play a significant role in building our attachment to things and bombard us with undemanding and shallow images of the ideal tarted up with glitz, sex, and violence. Our role is passive, not participatory: nothing is asked of us except that we consume.

More of us than ever before live without enduring attachments to other adults. In 1987, approximately 20 percent of the adult population were never married, compared to approximately 16 percent in 1970. People are marrying later than ever before. In 1956 men and women first married at the average ages of 22.5 and 20.2, respectively; the comparative ages in 1990 were 26.1 and 23.9 years.[20] In 1987, approximately 27 percent of families were headed by a single parent, compared to 21.6 percent in 1980. More children than ever before will be raised by only one parent. And even if we are raised by two parents, the chances are that both of them will be working, and our care will be relegated with more or less thought and planning to others, who are likely to have views about our moral, intellectual, and emotional development that differ from those of our parents. In 1988, 56.1 percent of women with children under six years of age were employed or seeking work, compared to 39 percent in 1975.[21] Many parents and children must cram the business of relating to one another into what has become known as "quality time"—the attenuated periods of child-parent interaction that occur at the end of the workday when tired and exhausted parents (16 percent of whom are single) can give their perhaps undivided but certainly frayed attention to their probably cranky and overly demanding children.[22]

Every year, fewer Americans are able to give service as volunteers in community organizations, no doubt reflecting the larger proportion of females in the work force. In 1987, 45 percent of Americans gave some kind of volunteer service compared to 52 percent in 1980.[23] These trends are evident in other kinds of civic behavior. For example, in 1984 only 60 percent of those registered to vote actually voted in the presidential election, compared to 68 percent in 1968.[24]

Given this attachment to things, our addiction to sensation, and our aloneness, how do we develop a sense of purpose to our lives? Things and television cannot provide a meaning to life sufficient to enable a human being to grow into a mature, loving, sharing, responsible adult. Nor can we expect the other adults who stand in as surrogate parents to our children while we are off at work to provide them with the emotional resources, values, beliefs, and morals that a healthy human must have. Under the best of conditions, these caretakers are supposed to practice with some degree of objectivity and prophylaxis: they should not become too intimately involved emotionally, morally, or spiritually with the children in their care. (Indeed, they dare not become involved with them physically in even the most innocent ways, lest they be reported as child abusers.)

Political leaders increasingly are presented to us on the television screen, their every move and utterance carefully orchestrated by handlers, their messages reduced to sound bites, and their public appearances chosen for being photo opportunities. Essentially, consumerism and sensation saturation dominate the communications from political leaders.

THE CHURCH OF INDIVIDUAL REPAIR

Some turn to the church to find a meaning and purpose to life (although church membership has been falling off).[25] The clergy presumably is available to help us enrich our spiritual lives; however, throughout the twentieth century, the clergy has lost its authority and capacity to carry out this function. The professional ministry has come to be concerned less and less with parishioners' spiritual lives and more and more with helping them deal with everyday problems of living. Today, men and women of the cloth dabble more heavily in psychotherapy, social action, and adult education than in such traditional activities as sermonizing about sin and saving souls.[26]

Ministers and priests have come to look and act more and more like psychotherapists, just as psychotherapists have come to look and act more and more like priests. These modern functions of the church reflect a great change in how it is perceived by society. It has come to pass that the church of the late twentieth century is, finally, in the self. Each person is a temple that he or she must sanctify and decorate and, most difficult of all, find for it a purpose and mission.

In earlier times, churches were great institutions located in impressive edifices with elaborate services and other ceremonial activities presided over by the clergy. More important, the church brought the community together and told people how to live and love, what was right and wrong, and how properly to raise a family. Today, the great task of helping individual persons to construct and administer their individual churches falls to psychotherapists. The established churches are now used primarily as social gathering places on Sundays and holidays, and psychotherapists have become secular priests and psychotherapy the modern-day church of individual repair. A dramatic illustration of this phenomenon was provided by the way Reverend Jimmy Swaggart's television ministry dealt with the national scandal that arose when knowledge of his personal and sexual problems became public. Swaggart was temporarily removed from his post while he was engaged in psychotherapy. There was much talk of how the preacher had injured his family and disappointed his followers but little comment about sin, perdition, and damnation.

The task of giving meaning to existence is an act of creation. The ability to create purposes and meanings to human existence is possessed by only a few great artists, philosophers, and religious leaders. Not many of us have the ability to create. For the vast majority of psychotherapists and their patients, it is a hopeless task for each to create his or her own church or temple. A few secular priests succeed at this, among them Carl Rogers, Fritz

Perls, Virginia Satir, and, of course, Freud. These creative therapists are like skilled shamans and priests, who create around
them troops of followers—both treaters and treated—who perceive them to be prophets and gurus.

Few of the followers, though, have the creative gift, and they
cannot maintain the momentum of the following after the creator
of the therapy leaves the scene. Thus, we witness the continuous
appearance and disappearance of new psychotherapies. (A 1980
publication lists more than 250 varieties of psychotherapy. No
doubt, the number is larger today.)[27] That is why many people
move so readily from one psychotherapist to another. Occasionally some lucky patients may, in their search for meaning and
purpose, stumble upon psychotherapists who help them find
happiness, purpose, or meaning. But psychotherapy is too much
like roulette at Monte Carlo—expensive and chancy—to serve as
a means for helping the suffering millions deal with the severe
social problems that are social work's concern.

THE SOCIAL FUNCTION OF POPULAR PSYCHOTHERAPY

Up through the nineteenth century, people believed that mental
illness was the result of invasive forces—external evil spirits and
demons. Toward the end of the 1800s, however, medical scholars
began to look at how men and women themselves brought on
these illnesses because of inner strains and conflicts, "nervousness," and neuroses. Freud's major contribution to modern
thought was freeing people to examine their own inner thoughts,
wishes, and impulses, no matter how infantile, sexual, and rebel-
lious. Freudian and other kinds of psychotherapies, most of them
offered in fifty-minute segments, constitute a neatly packaged
cure, one that is easily managed in a market-driven economy.

In the United States, psychoanalytic theory took a somewhat
different direction than it did in Europe. Psychotherapy in the
United States concerned itself more with self-expression and self-
realization than with self-discipline and self-control. By mid-

century, psychoanalysis had blended with other home-grown American therapies (for example, Rogerian-humanistic therapy, Gestalt therapy) and today represents a mix of Freud and various kinds of indigenous methods by which to cure anxiety, unhappiness, and stress.

Modern psychotherapy deals primarily with the aloneness of modern life; the absence of purpose and meaning in our lives; the difficulty of knowing who we are, how we should behave, what we deserve, and what our obligations are to others.[28] Having thrust off control of our lives by external agencies—the father, the state, the church, and intimate others—we are each of us left only with our self to which to turn to meet our emotional and psychic needs. One can hardly be more alone than that. Is it any wonder, then, that so many turn to professionals for guidance?

Some psychotherapists do deal with people who cannot carry out normal social and personal responsibilities, such as keeping themselves housed, clothed, and fed and fulfilling parental obligations. Nevertheless, many—perhaps a majority of—people who are seen by psychotherapists cannot be characterized as sick. Rather, they are "the worried well": middle-class young adults and young middle-aged, who are primarily professionals and primarily Caucasian, who are unhappy, unfulfilled, and unsatisfied.[29]

Moreover, it is not clear by any means that psychotherapy is the most effective means of treating even the truly ill. A great deal of evidence has accumulated that many people who are disabled by mental illness can be treated more effectively by socially structured treatments and communal experiences than by psychotherapy.[30] However, communal approaches to treatment have always been held suspect by Americans. We are the most individualistic nation in the world, a relatively young nation made up of a great mix of people. Many of us are still strangers to one another, still trying to figure out where we fit in and how best to deal with the dizzying assortment of American values, beliefs, and ideologies we confront, in addition to the great variety of skin colors and ethnic and religious backgrounds of which the American population is composed. This great assortment of people and ideas gives vitality to the American way of life but is also part of what makes us anxious, nervous, and uncertain—and therefore one of the reasons we seek the help of psychotherapists with such fervor.

There is nothing morally reprehensible about people seeking or offering psychotherapy on a private basis for the purpose of enhancing the individual's sense of self-esteem, acceptance, and well-being. However, there is cause for concern when public funds are used to support such programs and when concern for improving individual self-esteem and psychological well-being becomes a matter of public policy. This is the case in California, where the Task Force to Promote Self-Esteem and Personal and Social Responsibility was established in 1986.[31] The social implications of this development have been dramatized humorously by Garry Trudeau, creator of the "Doonesbury" comic strip.

The task force members, most of them psychotherapists, believe strongly that many societal problems can be eliminated by increasing individual self-esteem.[32] It will come as no surprise that the task force members think psychotherapists are the primary work force that will engineer this work. Apart from the fact that there is no evidence to support it, this proposition diverts public attention from important programs that meet basic human needs for child care, income maintenance, housing, and medical care and that simultaneously go a far longer way toward increasing people's self-esteem than individual psychotherapy. For example, parents have better feelings about themselves when their child is benefiting from good child care.

Our society's preoccupation with cultivation of the self is epidemic. Books such as *Looking Out for Number One* encourage the narcissism that is rampant in American society.[33] For example, it may surprise many readers to learn that 96 percent of all Americans suffer from "co-dependency," an affliction of the 1980s.[34] The term *co-dependence* is used to describe people who are unable to maintain "functional relationships"; it can be recognized by such symptoms as "thinking and feeling responsible for other people—for other people's feelings, thoughts, actions, choices, wants, needs, well-being, lack of well-being and ultimate destiny."[35] Thus, it appears that the virtues of caring for others, family obligations, and developing commitments are not only out of style but now are defined as pathological! The individual is left with only the church of the self for moral and emotional guidance. And if people are unable to construct or to enjoy these temples to onanism by themselves, the secular priests of the church of individual repair stand ready to assist—for a fee.

A large proportion of Americans have used and perceive of themselves as benefiting from psychotherapy, which now comprises a sizable work force. We can treat psychotherapy as a popular phenomenon, in fact—one that has pervaded popular culture and is used by and accessible to a majority of Americans.

Is "popular" an appropriate designation for psychotherapy? You will be easily persuaded by watching daytime television shows—the soaps, quiz shows, and especially, the "talk shows," the modern equivalent of the Roman circuses. There are two sets of gladiators: the individual persons who bare their breasts to the nation and the television audience. The breast-barers tell the audience intimate details of their lives: their emotions, disfigurements, eating habits, addictions, sexual behaviors, pathological personal relationships, and so forth. The more sordid, sad, and perverse the behaviors reported by the interviewees, the more rapt is the audience. After the victims have told their tales, the audience is invited to analyze them. Their unconscious motivations and fears are identified; their lack of morality and backbone may be pinpointed; their bravery may be admired; they may be given little homilies such as, "You only have one mother and no matter how bad she is you should love her."

To juice up the analysis, the talk show host brings on a champion gladiator/analyst, someone with expertise in probing around these kinds of problems, someone like Leo Buscaglia or Melodie Beattie.[36] These guests (who are usually promoting their latest book) go to the psychotherapeutic heart of the matter. They quickly identify "the child within" the victim, or the "untapped reservoir of love" in a relationship gone awry, or the unconscious "co-dependency" from which the victim suffers.

Psychotherapeutic analysis of self and others is both a major business and a popular entertainment. Americans are titillated by opportunities for (and opportunities to observe) the self-revelation, self-pity, and self-advertisement provided by psychotherapeutic modes of thinking. In watching these kinds of public encounters, one cannot help being impressed—and saddened—

by the sincere and genuine respect with which Americans have come to hold these ideas.

THE ORIGINS OF POPULAR PSYCHOTHERAPY

The common belief that popular psychotherapy in the United States dates back to Freud and to other European intellectual developments of the late nineteenth and early twentieth centuries is incorrect. Rather, the historical roots of popular psychotherapy lie in the great social movements of early nineteenth-century America, beginning approximately in the 1830s. The origins of popular psychotherapy are more American than Austrian; currently its public persona is more humanistic than psychoanalytic.

An understanding of the values, beliefs, and assumptions that guide the practice of the psychotherapeutic arts is required for an understanding of why social work has fallen captive to these practices. In the United States, popular psychotherapy had its beginnings in "mind cure" movements like phrenology, mesmerism, spiritualism, hydropathy, and electrotherapy.[37] Elements of these movements still exist in American life. We run, massage ourselves, and coddle, encourage, and cultivate our minds and bodies to achieve perfection and immortality. These strivings to make ourselves perfect and perfectly happy are continuations of the mind cures of the early nineteenth century, which were based on a powerful belief and hope in individual perfectibility to which Americans have a special affinity. There is a direct line of descent from the work of the mind curists to that of the positive thinkers, such as Norman Vincent Peale, Joshua Liebman, and Dale Carnegie, author of the world-famous book, *How to Win Friends and Influence People*.[38] (Carnegie's book had the most phenomenal success of any of the positive thinkers' works despite the fact that nowhere in it does he discuss friendship.)

Both movements—mind cure and positive thinking—were powerful in their time, and the popular psychotherapy of our day is partly rooted in them. Its other roots are in the mental hygiene movement early in the century, the power of the Freudian paradigm, which came into American life in the 1930s, and the influence that Carl Rogers and B. F. Skinner have had on how we perceive ourselves and how we behave.

Before World War II, psychology had been concerned almost exclusively with experiments and testing. In 1951, however, Carl Rogers introduced the idea of client-centered therapy and instituted a revolution.[39] When Rogers began his work, no university taught psychotherapy at all. Today psychotherapeutically oriented clinical psychologists dominate the field of psychology.[40]

We are not the first to write about the "psychotherapizing" of American society.[41] Among other work on the subject is *Habits of the Heart* by Robert Bellah and associates.[42] Their book is a sociological analysis of American community life that follows in a long line of community analyses going back to de Tocqueville's *Democracy in America* (1835) and including the Lynds' *Middletown* and *Middletown in Transition*.[43] *Habits of the Heart* is the first major book of that genre to include an analysis of psychotherapy as one of the central features of community life in America. Bellah and his associates say that "when Americans have difficulty operating within traditional relationships, as with marriage, they turn more and more to therapy." These authors see the significance of therapy as a "general outlook on life that has spread over the past few decades from a relatively small, educated elite to the middle-class mainstream of American life."[44]

All of the books we have cited in note 28 are essentially critiques of psychotherapy; they deal with such questions as how psychotherapy has affected social thought and behavior, the effectiveness (or ineffectiveness) of psychotherapy, and the scientific basis (or lack of such) for psychotherapeutic practice. Overall, the authors would agree that psychotherapy, and especially psychoanalysis, has been a major intellectual force in shaping minds, morals, and behaviors in the twentieth century, while, at the same time, they tend to be skeptical about the social value of psychotherapy, as well as claims of its effectiveness as a cure.

We share the skepticism of these authors about psychotherapy, but the subject is of interest to us only insofar as psychotherapy is becoming a replacement for social work and social welfare. As such, it has the potential to eliminate a profession dedicated to fostering the fragile sense of American communality. Its replacement by an institution that reflects the self-indulgence and radical individualism of American character should—at the least—not occur without notice.

THE ORIGINS OF SOCIAL WORK

Social work began in the 1890s as an outgrowth of the charities and corrections movement, which was based on a strongly held belief that society can be made wholesome by the application of scientific principles applied with love and kindness—a belief that has dwindled and atrophied over the course of a century. It is difficult now to envision the passion, commitment, and fervor of that movement.

The first Conference of Charities and Corrections was held in 1874.[45] The conference (as an organization) continued until 1983. (It became the National Conference of Social Work in 1917 and the National Conference on Social Welfare in 1957.) Social work as a profession began to take shape in 1883 as the result of the formation of Charity Organization Societies (COS), an effort to coordinate the charitable giving of voluntary alms to the poor. Their objectives, to eliminate "indiscriminate giving" and to "repress mendicancy," were met through a registry system whereby "friendly visitors" (most of them volunteers, especially middle- and upper-middle-class women) investigated applicants for charity and determined the applicants' "worthiness" and the nature of the help needed.[46]

The other important movement in charities and corrections was the social settlements. Settlement Houses, which first developed in England, were located in poor neighborhoods. Well-educated, upper-class men and women lived in them for the purpose of uplifting their neighbors morally, intellectually, and physically. Two remarkable American women, contemporaries, were associated with these two movements: Mary Richmond with the COS and Jane Addams with the Settlement Houses. Each shaped the development of social work as a profession.

Mary Richmond, a self-made person, formulated a systematic approach to friendly visiting that became known as social casework. She published extensively, developed educational programs, and almost succeeded in developing a national program of social services.

Jane Addams was a towering figure in her day—a woman of upper-class origins with a fine formal education. She was more a carrier of knowledge and value. Her Hull House Settlement in Chicago became an internationally famous institution, and she had a dramatic impact on the charities and corrections movement and the newly developing profession of social work.

Among her other achievements, Addams introduced the notion that a well-organized community life and culture can exist even among poor people and that one means by which to make society better is to attend to and nurture that community life and culture.[47] She implemented these ideas at Hull House dramatically, capturing worldwide attention. But as we look back now over a hundred years, we must conclude that social work has been shaped in neither Richmond's nor Addams's vision.

The term *social work* began to be used around the turn of the century. It started as the term "social works," used in much the same way as the more religious term "good works." Social work developed along the two lines laid out by Addams and Richmond—work with individual cases and work with communities—until 1919, when it discovered psychiatry. World War I had just ended, and there were lots of shell-shock victims to be treated. In addition, sexual hygiene, child guidance, and mental hygiene were new social movements and provided new arenas for social work practice.

This 1919 shift to psychiatry was the significant intellectual choice of the century for social work as a profession. Psychiatry became its guiding paradigm because social workers had nothing better they could do in the way of intervention to deal with their cases. You cannot do very much with sociology. It offers little in respect to managing face-to-face interaction with clients, and that is where psychiatry can be used. Thus, social workers needed something to do—an intervention. Psychiatry was available, and there was no one else to do it except physicians, who were concerned primarily with treating sick people. Moreover, the (mostly female) social workers were willing to serve as handmaidens to the (mostly male) physicians. Social workers thus took a psychiatric approach as their primary method of treatment and psychoanalysis as their primary source of theory.

From the 1920s to the 1950s, social workers' involvement in psychiatry was kept squarely under the control of physicians. Freud's "talking cure" provided a technology that social workers could use, but in the United States, the practice of psychoanalysis had been preempted by physicians, who continued to control the conditions under which social workers could practice psychotherapy until the 1950s.

Up to that time, any professional discussion of the relation between social workers and the practice of psychotherapy began with the assumption that psychiatric and psychoanalytic theory was the central core of social work knowledge. With that assumption, there remained only the task of dividing up the territory between social workers and psychiatrists. Today those discussions of the 1950s sound like so much hairsplitting. The following are examples:

> There is no qualitative difference [between casework and psychiatric therapy]. . . . The differences are quantitative. . . . The transference is probably handled more intensively by the psychoanalyst . . . than by the social workers.[48]

> "The psychoanalytic therapy . . . works with interpretations" while "nonanalytic psychotherapies do not.[49]

> While never *treating* unconscious material, the caseworker must be aware of how unconscious factors operate.[50]

This hairsplitting was meaningful in the context of the 1940s and 1950s because physicians did not willingly relinquish authority over psychotherapy.[51]

During the same period, humanistic psychology was emerging, providing the intellectual base from which social work and clinical psychology would undermine the hegemony of medicine over the psychotherapies. The gender conflict underlying this struggle was obvious; the members of the American Association of Psychiatric Social Workers were almost exclusively female, while psychiatry was a male-dominated profession. It was with the advent of humanistically oriented (nonmedically based) psychotherapy that social workers became free to practice the popular psychotherapies.

BUILDING A COMMUNITY-BASED SYSTEM OF SOCIAL CARE: A TWENTY-FIRST CENTURY MISSION FOR SOCIAL WORK

The objective of social work is to help people make use of social resources—family members, friends, neighbors, community organizations, social service agencies, and so forth—to solve their problems. Social workers deal with complex issues that involve questions of law (Who is entitled to receive social security and Medicare?), organizational roles (How is someone admitted to a nursing home? How does an agency provide services for the medically fragile children in their care?), and social policy (Should these children be placed in homes or in institutions?), as well as questions about human growth and development and behavioral dynamics. They deal with social problems, which concern the community, rather than personality problems of individuals. Helping individuals to make use of their social resources is one of the major functions of social work practice. And just as important is the social worker's function of developing and strengthening these resources by bringing people together in groups and organizations, by community education, and by organizational development.

Community social problems are increasing in both intensity and number, yet more and more professional social workers are becoming psychotherapists, and social work as a profession is devoting itself increasingly to the psychotherapeutic enterprise.[52] It is estimated that as many as 40 percent of the members of the National Association of Social Workers are in private practice for all or part of their work week.[53] Most of these professionals are engaged in what we shall refer to as the "popular psychotherapies."

The trend toward the private practice of psychotherapy in social work over the past sixty years has been quite dramatic. There was a beginning development of private practice in social work in the 1920s that all but disappeared as a result of the economic hardships of the Great Depression.[54] The private practice of social work began developing again in the 1950s, when only a small percentage of professionals was practicing privately. The number practicing privately grew to an estimated 13 percent by 1970, and, in 1990, to up to about 40 percent.[55] (We are referring here only to the percentages of professional social workers who practice psychotherapy privately. There are probably just as many who are employed by public and voluntary agencies whose major mode of practice is also psychotherapeutic.) Thus, if these trends continue over the next two or three decades, we can expect that social work will be engulfed entirely in the psychotherapy enterprise.

Many social-workers-turned-psychotherapists are defensive about their career choice—for example:

> Private practice is under attack again. . . . Social work schools and newsletters are bemoaning the fact that growing numbers of students—as many as 90 percent of those admitted to UCLA's program, for example—have private practice as their goal. Academics and administrators say that's a problem, and they attribute it to narcissism, self-interest and greed.[56]

"Why Do We Do It? It's Not for the Money—Honestly," is the title of a major editorial written by Robert L. Barker, the chief intellectual spokesman for the social work therapists, for the *Journal of Independent Social Work*.[57] We are not of the view that greed and self-interest are the chief motivations of the majority of social work psychotherapists, but there are exceptions. We recently received an announcement to social workers telling them how they could increase their incomes in private practice:

> Hi. My Name is Pete Buntman. Let me teach you how to double— and yes—even triple your income. . . . Let me help fill your waiting room with paying patients. My newsletter will help do it for you. And the cost—well I'm even offering you a *Special Discount Offer—Save $100*.[58]

The rest of the five-page letter from Mr. Buntman (M.S.W., LCSW.) is filled with promises of gifts to those who subscribe to his newsletter, as well as a few tips on how to become rich through private practice—for example: "I recognized early on that Medicaid patients, patients on welfare—patients who couldn't afford my services—would never help me support my family."

Many graduate schools of social work in the United States, moreover, educate the majority of their students to be psychotherapists.[59] Most of these students will go into private practice. In 1984, Hans S. Falck, editor of *Journal of Education for Social Work*, wrote:

> In offering courses in social work therapy, schools have opened the door to private practice, to third party reimbursement, to limited private practice, taking the cream off the top as far as fee-paying clients are concerned, leaving the masses of the poor, the chronically ill, the multiproblem families to find help and support through underfunded community agencies. And this means there is no one to attend to *their* welfare.[60]

Falk believes, as we do, that the community should not pay for this kind of education for social work: "If people want to become private practitioners of social work, fine, but then let them pay *fully* for their education."

The important issue here is not how private practitioners are paid but, rather, what they do. Private practitioners usually provide various forms of psychotherapy to a fairly well-off population that some have characterized as the "worried well." Agency-based professionals deal with more low-income and minority people and with more children; they make greater use of community resources and are more likely to refer service users to a wide range of other services.[61]

Increasingly, social work positions in the publicly supported social services and community-based nonprofit agencies are filled by people who have, at best, only bachelor's-level training in social work.[62] And many higher-level administrative and supervisory positions in the public services require a clinical social work license, a requirement that is inappropriate for the public social services and further psychotherapizes public services.

Professions are usually incapable of self-reform. Most estab-

lished professionals, professional educators, and agency administrators have too much of their lives invested in the status quo to
risk big changes. Most of them have, after all, experienced professional, financial, and social success in their practice and are un-
derstandably reluctant to give up a psychotherapeutic bird in the
hand for a community-based system of social care in the bush.

Professions will not change unless the public helps them to.
Policymakers and legislators acting for the public can choose to
pay for certain kinds of services and certain kinds of education
and not others; they can choose to license certain practices and
not others. In our concluding chapter, we recommend some policies for social work and psychotherapy that we believe will
serve the public interest. We hope that our position will generate
thoughtful debate.

That debate should start with a clarification of the difference
between social work and psychotherapy. The major function of
social work is concerned with helping people perform their normal life tasks by providing information and knowledge, social
support, social skills, and social opportunities; it is also concerned with helping people deal with interference and abuse
from other individuals and groups, with physical and mental disabilities, and with overburdening responsibilities they have for
others. Most important, social work's objective is to strengthen
the community's capacities to solve problems through development of groups and organizations, community education, and
community systems of governance and control over systems of
social care. The concern of psychotherapy is with helping people
to deal with feelings, perceptions, and emotions that prevent
them from performing their normal life tasks because of impairment or insufficient development of emotional and cognitive
functions that are intimately related to the self. Social workers
help people make use of and develop community and social resources to build connections with others and reduce alienation
and isolation; psychotherapists help people to alter, reconstruct,
and improve the self.

We must, if we desire to give direction to the professions of
social work and psychotherapy, take on the difficult task of
drawing boundaries. This can be a painful task, especially for social workers who are eager to be all things to all people, because

it requires that priorities be established. Some functions and practices must be excluded from their professional sphere, no matter how socially desirable and attractive, because they are diversionary and subversive to their major mission. Our central point is that the popular psychotherapies have diverted social work from its original mission and vision of the perfectibility of society.

There is a yet unfulfilled mission for social work: to deal with the enormous social problems under which our society staggers—the social isolation of the aged, the anomie experienced by youth, the neglect and abuse of children, homelessness, drug addiction, and the problems of those who suffer from AIDS. Psychotherapy is useless in dealing with these great social problems.

Social work's mission should be to build a meaning, a purpose, and a sense of obligation for the community. It is only by creating a community that we establish a basis for commitment, obligation, and social support. We must build communities that are excited about their child care systems, that find it exhilarating to care for the mentally ill and the frail aged, that make demands upon people to behave, to contribute, and to care for one another. Psychotherapy will not enable us to do that, and the further down the psychotherapeutic path social workers go, the less effective they will be in achieving their true mission. There are models for doing this. The Civilian Conservation Corps of the 1930s, the War on Poverty of the 1960s, the wide variety of self-help groups, the civil rights movement, the Peace Corps, and the National Service Corps, now being discussed in Congress, are all models by which we can build communities that change people, give purpose and meaning to peoples' lives, and enable us to care about and love one another. To accept this as their professional mission requires that social workers make a great change in their way of thinking and their way of practicing.

This is a task that is tantamount to the cleaning of the Augean stables. We have, all of us, professionals and laypersons alike, been socialized to think and act in psychotherapeutic terms and to prize one-on-one interventions. Social workers educate their students to follow suit. It is not surprising that students also prize the psychotherapeutic role. Social services—public, voluntary, and for profit—are organized to make individualized psychotherapeutic forms of helping the most significant we have to offer. Whether dealing with child abuse and neglect, addictions, loneliness, anxiety, economic dependency, or other physical and mental disabilities, it is psychotherapeutically oriented work with individuals that is considered to be the key.

Social workers generally look at use of groups, community associations, and voluntary associations as of secondary importance to change. At best, they provide "social support" and "helping networks"; somewhat less importantly, they are good information resources and recreational experiences, and they provide respite for caregivers and backups and reinforcement for individual treatment.

There are occasional episodes—usually times of national crises—when social workers rediscover the group and the community. This occurred during the two world wars, the Great Depression, and the civil rights revolution. But when the crises subside, social workers return quickly to individualized therapy as the preferred means for dealing with social problems. When there are cuts in allocations for social programs, social agencies retreat unhappily to offering group treatment in place of psychotherapy. They perceive these communally organized substitutes for "the real thing" as inferior.

Professionals have these perceptions of social treatments because their belief in the individual's capacity for change is so strong and their faith in the power of the group and community is so weak. It will require a very great change in the profession, in professional education, in the organization of our service systems, and, most of all, in our systems of belief for social work to provide the community with a social program to deal with social problems.

It may be too late. Social workers have been socialized for more than seventy years to believe that psychiatry, psychoanalysis, and humanistic psychology are appropriate means for dealing with social problems. The profession is in the process of being engulfed by popular psychotherapy. Social workers must differentiate between these two practices and stop deluding themselves into believing that they are not different. Social workers should not be secular priests in the church of individual repair; they should be the caretakers of the conscience of the community.

They should not ask, "Does it feel good to *you?*" They should help communities create good. There must be a profession that provides a vision that enables us to direct our energies to the creation of healthy communities.

In the last two chapters of the book, we present a reformulation of theory for social work practice and a plan for development of a national system of community-based social care. We call for a social work practice that abandons individually oriented psychotherapeutic work and develops an adult education approach to helping people solve their problems. This approach will empower users of social services instead of making them dependent on psychotherapists and infantilizing them. Moreover, it will foster communality, and in the long run it will lead to a community-based system of social care far more efficient and effective than what we now have.

CHAPTER TWO

PSYCHOTHERAPY

Magic, Religion, or Science?

———◆◆◆———

The television screen lights up with the image of a man pacing back and forth in a room of uncertain dimensions. He is sharing what seem to be his deepest hopes and concerns with another man who listens intently from across a desk: "All I did was build a computer. Next thing I know, I own a company. The stock splits. I make a ton of money! I guess along the way I turned into a real jerk. I just want to simplify things, you know? Get my values back. That's why I'm here." At this point the viewer expects the man behind the desk to offer some kind of insight into the other man's plight or to ask a clarifying question. And why not? It seems obvious to anyone familiar with American culture that the man behind the desk is one of our modern-day secular priests to whom one turns with such perplexing problems: a psychotherapist. To our surprise and amusement, however, the camera then opens up a larger perspective of the scene, and we discover that this is not a psychotherapist's office but an automobile dealership. The car salesman/therapist speaks: "I think you're doing the right thing. Now, based on those feelings, are we talking two doors, or four?"

The joke is on us. The troubled man has not really sought out a therapeutic relationship but has turned to the other place that Americans search for "values," the marketplace. The implication is that his purchase of a small, more utilitarian car will somehow facilitate his return to a more authentic self. The advertising executive knows that the identification of purchaser with purchase contributes significantly to creating demand for any product. Consumption can be (ought to be?) therapeutic. Similarly, therapy is surely, as Joel Kovel has noted, "quite eligible for commodification."[1] A Fortune 500 marketing expert could not have done a better job than Freud with the "fifty-minute hour" or the humanistic psychotherapists and their "weekend intensives" in developing a product to satisfy the commodity fetishism of our times.

The presence of the therapeutic theme in a television car commercial helps illustrate the ubiquitous nature of modern psychotherapy, as well as its adaptation to the market economy. Another aspect of American psychotherapy as a social phenomenon is present but less obvious in our example. Psychotherapy, in form and substance, tends to locate the source of problems within the individual. The "client" in our example did not elaborate the ways in which the social relations encountered in owning a company and becoming rich might have helped to turn him into a "jerk." Furthermore his solution, whether psychotherapeutic or consumer therapeutic, would have been an individual one.

The point is more obvious if the social conditions for the client are changed a bit. Consider the scenario of a woman who brings the following story to the man behind the desk:

> I used to have a pretty good life: married, healthy kids, and a good job. But then the factory shut down, my husband was laid off and started drinking. One thing led to another; we lost our home, he left us, my income couldn't cover day care, and my absences from work cost me my job. Feeling overwhelmed, I started drinking and neglecting my kids. I guess along the way I turned into a real jerk. I just want to simplify things, you know? Get my kids back. That's why I'm here.

This would not make for a very good car advertisement. On the other hand, although the woman's problems might reasonably be considered as significantly influenced by the social conditions in which they developed, it would not surprise us to learn that she sought the help of a psychotherapist. After all, these problems could easily be interpreted in modern American society as a consequence of individual character deficiencies amenable to correction through the medium of a therapeutic relationship. This woman would not benefit from the same high-priced therapeutic counsel as the wealthy man in search of his values. She would most likely be involved in court-ordered reunification counseling in order to regain custody of her children. The purveyor of this therapy (quite likely a social worker) would probably be unable to provide the social services necessary to deal with the social conditions contributing to the woman's problems—day care, substance abuse treatment, housing, job placement—but would gladly offer a "talking cure." Perhaps this would result in the woman's being happier, but it is unlikely to solve her problems.

In this chapter we explore the characteristics of psychotherapy in America and how it has evolved. We are primarily interested in the role psychotherapy plays in our society in order to compare this to our vision of the proper role of the profession of social work. To understand how social work has been derailed from its original mission we must understand the powerful position psychotherapy has gained as a social institution and the privileged status its practitioners enjoy.[2]

We will find that psychotherapy has increasingly replaced our reliance on magic and faith in organizing our experience of the world. In the process, psychotherapy has come to reinforce a particularly American faith in the perfectibility of the individual, thereby contributing to our tendency to treat public issues as private troubles.

MAGIC, RELIGION, AND SCIENCE: THE LONG ROAD TO MODERN PSYCHOTHERAPY

Historians have outlined the ways in which magic and religious faith have served the purpose throughout history of countering psychological pain. In many ways, psychotherapy has come to fill a void created by the inability of these social institutions to continue to meet the emotional needs of people in Western cultures.

In spite of the fact that magic and faith still have a hold on large segments of the American public, there has been a gradual shift over time in the dominant worldview and its corresponding mode of healing. Over approximately two thousand years, the "civilized world in its healing methods replaced magic by faith, and faith by science."[3] In fact, as the institutional manifestation of the "scientific" approach to psychic healing, psychotherapy has become the heir of magic and faith.

The attribution of causality is an aspect of our individual and collective views of the world that plays a central role in the type of therapeutic approach used in a given culture and its efficacy. The answer to the question, What causes me to do what I do? has been part and parcel of every therapeutic technique ever used.[4] Moreover, the dominant worldview includes explanations for the acts of others as well. Our view of the world contributes decisively to our understanding of the failures of ourselves and others. Do we attribute them to possession by evil spirits, a lack of faith, or individual psychopathology?

Magical thinking is a central characteristic of cultures in which the dominant assumptive system attributes the cause of suffering to supernatural forces. Faced with a fearsome and incomprehensible world, the believer seeks the power of magical omnipotence. The amulet and talisman of the magician become for users the power that will protect them from harm, physical or psychological, and the magician becomes a human bridge between the worlds of spirits and objects. No act of faith is required on the part of one who lives in a magical world since belief in magic is uncritical by nature.

A culture that has a dominant worldview steeped in religious faith requires more of the believer.[5] Magic may be distinguished from faith by noting that the faithful give up their magical quest for omnipotence by renunciation of their "selfish desires and interests in return for salvation."[6] Those whose worldview gives much importance to supernatural forces and the magical science associated with the control of these forces do not abandon this position easily. The Catholic church, for example, has had considerable difficulty convincing the masses of their need for salvation.

Historically the church has gone to great lengths in its attempts to eradicate various manifestations of magical science, most notably during the Inquisition, when the heretics who suffered the most were accused witches. The persecution of witches was not simply an effort to drive out the possessed or evil but was perceived by the Inquisitors as a struggle over the hearts and minds of the people—an attempt to reconstruct their view of the world. In his comparison of the Inquisition to the mental health movement, Thomas Szasz has emphasized that the so-called good witches of the period were more likely to be persecuted than the "evil witches" because they were a more potent enemy in the struggle over the loyalty of the populace. As effective "therapists" they were more of a threat to the psychical hegemony of the priests.[7] The example of the Inquisition's persecution of witchcraft offers an interesting context for the understanding of more recent conflicts, such as the battle between psychiatry and psychoanalysis early in this century and the current battles for turf among the various professional groups (psychiatrists, psychologists, marriage and family counselors, and social workers) laying claim to psychotherapeutic privileges. Who will be the new priests?

Developments in Western science during the seventeenth century would see the wheels of history turning in a direction that would ultimately render the practitioner of magic an insignificant threat to the church and religious faith generally in comparison to the new priesthood of the scientists. Over the course of a century, the worldview of educated people evolved from an essentially medieval perspective to one that was essentially modern.[8] Seventeenth-century science contrasted with both the magical and religious worldviews. The emergence of the natural laws of science (particularly physics) resulted in the elimination of animism as a credible method of explaining actions in the world. Newton's First Law of Motion held that matter was lifeless and the solar system operated on its own momentum without the need for divine intervention. Furthermore, the change in humanity's place in the universe left little significance to the notion of religious purpose. While the earth and human endeavor were the center of all things in medieval times, the discoveries of Galileo, Descartes, Newton, and Leibniz, among others, made it seem "unlikely that this immense apparatus was designed for the good of certain small creatures on this pin-point."[9]

Magic and faith still play a role in the lives of many people today, particularly in terms of their approach to the amelioration of psychic pain. Conversely, primitive peoples do not live on magic alone; they know and make use of many qualities of the natural world. In essence, "primitive" peoples are so only part of the time, just as we moderns are not as "civilized" as we often believe.[10] As we have already seen in the example of the conflict between Christianity and witchcraft, our ambivalence concerning the true nature of the troubles we face has had an impact upon the types of healers we choose. That ambivalence continues to be reflected in the schools of modern psychotherapy that rely on a spiritual foundation.

The scientific discoveries of the seventeenth century altered the perspective of most of the educated population in Europe and America but did not change their preferred source of solace overnight. Indeed, it would be two hundred years before Freud would develop the metapsychology and clinical method of his psychoanalysis, and even longer for those discoveries to lead to a movement of psychic healers (the psychoanalysts) and an opposition (transpersonal therapists, humanistic psychologists, and behaviorists).

FAITH, INDIVIDUALISM, AND THE AMERICAN WAY OF MENTAL HEALING

The nineteenth century saw the development of numerous pseudosciences and what sociologist Robert Bellah and his associates have referred to as a "combination of popular psychology and vaguely spiritual religiosity."[11] Both movements foreshadow the American version of the psychotherapeutic worldview. We will examine one of the pseudosciences, phrenology, as well as the "pop psychology" of the period.

Phrenology had its origins in the anatomic work done by the Viennese physician Franz Gall in the late eighteenth and early nineteenth centuries.[12] After discovering that the folds of gray and white matter in the human brain have a specific structural relationship, Gall hypothesized that this structure has a meaning. He postulated that certain areas of the brain have specific relationships with various human "propensities," "sentiments," and "faculties."

Gall's ideas were a significant contribution to the development of clinical neurology in his day. Unfortunately, his work received greater popular acclaim as a result of the growth of a somewhat less scientific endeavor, phrenology, probably best remembered for the amusing "maps" of the skull that laid out the topography of all human traits and propensities. In America, phrenology created great interest as a parlor game, a practical method of predicting the success of relationships, a means of diagnosing mental ailments, and a basis for restructuring school curricula in order to "improve the race."[13]

Phrenologists did not limit themselves to diagnosis and prediction. Soon they were engaged in direct influence of their subjects through applying pressure to the various "organs" or phrenological bumps on their skulls. Generally, the curative agent was believed to be the phrenologist's manipulation of some form of magnetic force. Many subjects were eager to have their propensities "balanced" through this phrenomagnetic therapy. An important characteristic of this form of healing—one that is common to other American pseudosciences—is the breadth of problems the phrenologists claimed to be able to solve. Almost any human difficulty was believed to be amenable to amelioration through the use of this technique.

Phrenology was only one of a host of hybrid sciences to become popular in nineteenth-century America. Other related movements were mesmerism, spiritualism, electrotherapy, and hydrotherapy.[14]

When one speaks of these earlier mind cures, the emphasis is on the latter word—*cures.* Early nineteenth-century medicine was a harsh business.[15] Surgery was known as the "brutal craft," being almost invariably a death sentence; medical care in general was life threatening; and women were much more likely than men to be its victims. Infant mortality and death from childbirth were common phenomena. As an alternative to the medical science of the times, the mind cures were very appealing, and especially so to women. Moreover, the mind cures opened new careers to women such as Mary Baker Eddy, founder of Christian Science.

These movements were more than a reaction to nineteenth-century medical practice. The desire for perfection of one's temperament—apparent in the popularity of phrenology—had much to do with the growth of mind cures and faith healing and has much in common with that which brings many moderns into psychotherapy.

These movements grew in the context of developments in religion and philosophy and the popularization of science. Early in the century, religious revivalism was on the rise as the constraints of puritanism began to give way, and the dispersed populace of the countryside was exhorted to engage in personal experiences of salvation. In New England, romantic transcendentalism, which contained the belief that the human mind and soul are manifestations of God, only temporarily dwelling in the world of flesh and matter, began to hold sway. The implications were considerable:

> Reunion with God, the mystic return to God, was the supreme conclusion of life. Moreover, it meant a reflection of perfectionism and a life of triumph over matter, which itself was imperfection. ... Such a philosophy shaped a plan for mental and physical life, for a religion and for a philosophy of mental healing. ... Those who absorbed these concepts felt buoyant.[16]

This "buoyancy" of the spirit of nineteenth-century Americans, combined with a rather loose notion of science, created a fertile field of faith in which a host of hypnotists, spiritualists, food faddists, and other self-appointed healers planted the seeds of their fantastic ideas. The essential message of these faith healers was that if one only believed hard enough, anything was possible.

As the century progressed, various quasi-religions that loosely shared an idealism concerning the power of mind over matter gained popularity. Mary Baker Eddy's Christian Science is interesting because of its lasting success.[17] Eddy developed a religious idealism she called the Science of Christ, which holds that God is the essence of everything, Spirit the only reality of consequence, and that matter does not exist. If the believer could dispense with any concern for the material plane, physical illness would disappear. Furthermore, the discipline of the mind she was espousing held out the promise of a cure for all mental disease.

Eddy's project was the delineation of a therapeutic ideology that she believed could be taught to others. In fact, she had great success in that endeavor; many of her students taught her methods in both the United States and throughout Asia and Europe. The growth of Eddy's church between 1890 and 1910 was so great that it led Mark Twain, a critic of Christian Science, to fear that by 1930 there would be a "politically formidable" body of 30 million Christian Scientists.[18] Although not quite as successful as Twain feared, Eddy's project did sell millions of books and pamphlets, provided the therapy of choice for millions of Americans over several decades, and continues to maintain a following today.

Christian Science entailed a set of beliefs that any individual could learn and it was of necessity an individual commitment that would realize the cure. These two characteristics—an act of individual effort and a method that could be taught—make Christian Science a progenitor of most modern pop psychology.

Although the popular power of the mind cures began to wane at the turn of the century, the ideological theme that they reflected was maintained in the work of the positive thinkers, whose work is somewhat more familiar to many of us.[19] The positive thinkers were less concerned with physical cures and more with the power of positive thinking to help the individual achieve peace of mind and success. Readers will recognize here the words of Norman Vincent Peale, Joshua Liebman, and Dale Carnegie, our contemporaries.[20] The great intellectual positive thinkers were William James, Harry Emerson Fosdick, and George Beard. More contemporary examples of this tradition include Werner Erhard's EST (Erhard Seminars Training) and the lasting success of L. Ron Hubbard's Church of Scientology and his "science of the mind."[21]

Individualism was enough a part of nineteenth-century America to lead de Tocqueville, the outsider, to coin the phrase, and Emerson, the insider, to pen his ode to nonconformity, "Self-Reliance."[22] It was in the context of transcendentalist and frontier individualism that the peculiar American attraction to faith healing and the power of mind over matter took root. Bellah and his associates use the term *expressive individualism* to describe the notion that "each person has a unique core of feeling and intuition that should unfold or be expressed if individuality is to be realized," as well as the possibility of the individualist "to 'merge' with other persons, with nature, or with the cosmos as a whole."[23] They also conclude that this philosophy has much in common with the twentieth-century culture of psychotherapy.

Expressive individualism, combined with the increasing pace, competitiveness, and transitory quality of life, created new forms of mental illness for many Americans. The physician George Beard coined the term *neurasthenia* to describe a generalized nervous exhaustion that seemed to be plaguing millions of Americans in the late 1800s. He and others attributed the new illness to various characteristics of "modern civilization," such as business competition, rapid change in ideas, and a fast-paced social life.[24]

In fact, the mind cure and positive-thinking movements of the nineteenth century were largely a response to the inability of institutions to fulfill the purposes they once served. As Bellah and associates point out:

> Whether the treatment offered was increased will power, a rest cure, or reliance on the Power of the Infinite, it was offered to the anxious middle-class individual for whom ties of kinship, religious fellowship, and civic friendship were no longer, or no longer sufficiently adequate to provide psychic support. The support that traditional relationships no longer adequately supplied to the overburdened individual now came in the form of new institutions.[25]

An implicit belief in individual perfectibility through solitary effort directed upon the self, so characteristic of nineteenth-century treatment for psychic ills, remains an essential component of modern American culture and psychotherapy.

Adherence to expressive individualist ideology not only leads to an inward search for solutions to one's problems; it also tends to narrow one's focus when considering the problems of others. The words of no less an exponent of individualism than Emerson himself provide an example of this dark side of expressive individualism and its relation to social work ethics:

> Are they *my* peer? I tell thee, thou foolish philanthropist, that I grudge the dollar, the dime, the cent I give to such men as do not belong to me and to whom I do not belong. There is a class of persons to whom by all spiritual affinity I am bought and sold; for

them I will go to prison, if need be; but your miscellaneous popular charities; the education at college of fools; the building of meeting-houses to the vain and to which many now stand; alms to sots; and the thousandfold Relief Societies;—though I confess with shame I sometimes succumb and give a dollar, it is a wicked dollar, which by and by I shall have the manhood to withhold.[26]

It appears that the reluctance of the welfare state has deep roots in American culture.

Although the persistence of the forms of healing described is a testament to the ability of the worldviews they reflect to organize and explain human experience, it is also obvious that most modern psychotherapy aspires to be a more rational and scientific approach.

PSYCHOTHERAPY IN THE TWENTIETH CENTURY: AN INDIVIDUAL OR COMMUNAL ETHOS?

If the growth of faith healing and positive thinking in the nineteenth century was partly a symptom of the failure of traditional communal social institutions to ameliorate psychic stress, then our century, with the growth of the new institution of psychotherapy, might be considered the era in which this failure was rendered complete. The past one hundred years have seen what sociologist Phillip Rieff describes as the abandonment of the "positive communities" of past cultural forms for the "negative communities" of today.[27]

Rieff discusses how cultures, which change over time, contribute to the constitution of the worldviews of their members. All cultures have a therapeutic function, insofar as they are systems of symbolic integration—whether these systems are called religion, philosophy, ideology, psychotherapy, or any other name.[28] A culture is particularly therapeutic if it is compelling enough to introduce a character ideal.[29] Of course, a given culture can fall prey to another one that is more capable of fulfilling the therapeutic integrative function.

For Rieff, the history of Western culture up to this century is one of the development of various "positive communities"—that is, they offer some sort of salvation of the self, experienced through a transformative process by which all personal relations are made subordinate to agreed-upon communal purposes. The positive community offers the individual an explanation of both good times and bad times in terms of a shared structure of meaning and purpose. This is a quality shared by animist cults of the third century, the Catholic church for much of the last two thousand years, groups of faith healers in the last century, and youth gangs and twelve-step groups today.

Rieff argues that the modern era has seen the development in advanced industrialized countries of negative communities. The individual member of a negative community does not seek salvation through the group. Whatever sense this person makes of his or her life and the social relationships on which it is based is essentially an individual task. This character ideal Rieff has termed the "therapeutic."

We do not see the ongoing abandonment of the positive communities of the past as bad things in and of themselves. There is much to recommend a rational and scientific understanding of the human condition. On the other hand, the so-called triumph of the therapeutic may be contributing to a situation in which we have lost our ability to conceive of communal solutions even for social problems.

Thus far, we have touched on a few major historical developments in order to make sense of the background of the various denominations of what we have referred to as the church of individual repair. We will now compare and contrast the work of certain individuals and movements that have helped shape psychotherapy in the twentieth century.

Sigmund Freud's psychoanalysis is a good place to begin an examination of twentieth-century psychotherapy, not only because of its seminal relationship to many other approaches but also because it represents a radical change from the therapies of the past. Many might argue that Freud's work does not constitute an adequate science of the human psyche, but few would dispute that it was a significant break from the religious and communal therapies of his day. Freud was a confirmed atheist, and faith healing was not in his repertoire of clinical aids. His notion of unconscious determinism was incompatible with any magic of human omnipotence. Freud argued that civilization and its institutions, while providing useful constraints on humanity's inherent aggressive and self-satisfying tendencies, also require of members individual renouncement and the guilt that accompanies it. For Freud, the family is the stage upon which the oedipal drama takes places; the oedipal conflict is the primary grist for the analytic mill. He had little faith in the possible construction of a workable positive community but instead was working for the end of an "illusion."

Freud's clinical method, psychoanalysis, reflected this lack of reliance on a communal symbolic system. In place of such a system, the analyst was to help strengthen the patient's ego in order for it to deal as a "frontier creature" with the conflicting demands of the id, superego, and reality.[30] American ego psychology later focused much attention on the autonomous qualities of the ego, emphasizing the importance of strengthening these aspects of the patient's psyche.[31] Ultimately, the analytic search for the truth of the patient's symptoms, the truth that leads to the termination of analysis, is the responsibility of the analysand.

Rieff makes a useful distinction between what he calls "therapies of commitment" and "analytic therapies."[32] He argues that the lasting significance of Freud's work is partly a function of its appropriateness to his time (and ours). In this view, Freud's psychoanalysis was developed as an alternative to preceding therapies of commitment, which had become inadequate. According to Rieff, analytic therapies are most appropriate for persons living in an individualistic and democratic culture. He delineates the differences between the two types of therapies in the following way:

> Analytic therapies . . . arise in an historical period concomitant with the rise of democratic individualism. Commitment therapies, however, operate by returning the individual to the cosset of his natal community or by retraining him for membership in a new community, with a more effective pattern of symbolic integration. . . . Analytic therapies, on the other hand, are uniquely modern and depend largely upon Freudian presuppositions. The therapeutic effort is not primarily transformative but informative. The

assumption of the analytic theory is that there is no positive community standing behind the therapist.[33]

Seen in this light, Freudian psychoanalysis seems like the perfect therapeutic vehicle for our times. The "autonomous frontier creature" of psychoanalysis thrives in the cultural context of expressive individualism.

Many other approaches to psychotherapy have developed since Freudian thought reached our shores, and some have had considerable success, outshining even psychoanalytic psychotherapy for periods of time. One of these approaches, given impetus by the work of Carl Jung, is transpersonal psychotherapy, which emphasizes the spiritual aspect of human existence.

If Freud's work was an attempt at creating a therapy that would help to complete the collapse of the Christian myth, then Jung (who differed with Freud over the issue of spirituality) and other transpersonal therapists can be seen as those who would attempt to resurrect the usefulness of myth. Jung attempted to create a metareligion that draws upon all of the world's religious mythology. He believed that the "collective unconscious" is manifested in all religious symbolism.[34] The individual who enters therapy with a Jungian analyst seeks to "individuate" through the process of creating his or her own mythology.[35] Ironically, the process of individuation is the creation of a personal religion that springs from a notion of communal faith exemplified by the collective unconscious. In general, transpersonal therapies seek to help the individual recognize the way in which he or she is trying to become an organic part of something that is greater than the self and, ultimately, to help the person achieve that unity. These are therapies of commitment in the sense that Rieff uses that term.

Transpersonal therapies are also consistent with Bellah's definition of expressive individualism since they focus on individuation while offering the possibility of a transcendental merging with some greater spiritual realm. Furthermore, they direct scant attention to the possible social contributors to human misery.

Behaviorism was clearly the dominant force in American academic psychology for the first half of this century and in its various forms (e.g., social learning theory and cognitive behaviorism) still dominates that realm, although to a lesser degree.[36] The followers of Ivan Pavlov, John Watson, J. Wolpe, and then B. F. Skinner applied their learning theory in a number of ways, primarily in the field of education. Some of them developed behavior therapies that have been used to address various problems of individuals—particularly phobias and addictions—and behavior modification techniques have become a fixture in many therapeutic milieu settings for children and adults.

The philosophical underpinnings of behaviorism are more or less compatible with those of Newton and Darwin. According to the behaviorist perspective, human beings are products of their environment in that they are either conditioned or learn to behave in certain ways. Both the notions of the unique subjectivity of human beings and their innate spiritual nature (ideas central to many other psychotherapeutic approaches) are considered by bdhaviorists to be explanatory fictions. In this sense, behavioral therapies are at least as radical a departure from past therapies of commitment as Freudian psychoanalysis.

Behavioral therapy has never attracted hordes of devotees in the same way as psychoanalysis, transpersonal therapies, and humanistic psychology. Americans do not like to consider themselves motivationally on a par with mice. On the other hand, mass market books and treatment programs focusing on diets and fitness often suggest different ways to "reward yourself" for desired behavior. In this sense, behaviorism contributes to the American myth of individual perfectibility.

In the United States, humanistic psychology developed as a third force in response to behaviorism and the psychoanalytic tradition.[37] Humanistic psychologists faulted the other schools for being too reductive and mechanistic, reflecting a long-standing philosophical debate among psychologists and clinicians over the reduction of psychology to the status of a natural science.[38] Drawing on a number of sources, the humanistic psychologists launched an attack on "the mechanomorphic model of man being forged by the psychology of their day," eventually creating a formal movement of humanistic psychology in America by the 1950s.[39]

It is probably impossible to provide a precise definition of humanistic psychology. It is somewhat easier to describe what it is not, particularly since the humanistic school has been described at times as a "protest movement."[40] It seems to be directed against the Newtonian and Darwinian models of humans, the positivistic orientation of academic psychology since Hobbes and Locke, and the generally "mechanistic, deterministic, and reductionist character" of that psychology.[41]

Humanistic psychology's emphasis on the uniqueness of each individual's experience and the client-centered methods of counseling Rogers developed have had a significant impact on the conduct of psychotherapy in this country. Most clinicians have been exposed to these ideas, and much introductory training in psychotherapeutic technique (such as "reflective listening") borrows heavily from Rogers's work.

In the case of humanistic psychology, it is particularly important to distinguish between the intellectual movement and its many social manifestations, such as encounter groups, sensitivity training, and the revival-like workshops of the human potential gurus.[42] Given the qualities of the American character that we have already described, it is easy to see how humanistic psychology blossomed into a "human potential movement" for the middle and upper classes, who, following Abraham Maslow's hierarchy of human needs, were the only Americans ready for and able to finance such self-actualization.

It would seem at first glance that humanistic psychotherapy is anything but a therapy of commitment. Indeed, the Me Generation (which we believe has actually become a multigenerational group) has not been notable for its large-scale construction of community.[43] The focus on the centrality of individual experience—that all one need do is "feel"—is a perfect reflection of the philosophy of expressive individualism.

On the other hand, it may still be the case that Americans cannot live by expression alone. Many humanists found something wanting in the boundless individual freedom suggested by the new movement and increasingly moved in a transpersonal direction. Maslow himself hoped that this would be the eventual destination of psychology.[44]

The development of family therapy is worth mentioning because of the relatively unique way that the family therapist defines the client. Family therapists generally focus on the family as the unit of treatment rather than any individual in the family. Therapists and academics from a wide range of disciplines have contributed to the development of the various approaches that are loosely referred to as family therapy.[45] Implicit in all of these perspectives is the idea that the family can be the source of psychological dysfunction in any of its members, and therefore the examination of family dynamics should be considered as an essential part of the therapeutic process. More fundamentally, family therapy theorists have been at the forefront of efforts to place individual human behavior in an interpersonal and social context, arguing that human behavior and experience cannot possibly be understood when removed from this larger context.[46] Some group therapies rely on this same understanding. Although this fact is not explicit in all schools of family or group therapy, most such approaches are essentially therapies of commitment where the family or group itself is to some extent the community to which the individual commits himself or herself. However, because of the attention these therapeutic approaches pay to the social context of human behavior and experience, they stand in stark contrast to the expressive individualist tendency found in most other modern therapies of commitment.

PERSPECTIVES ON PSYCHOTHERAPY TODAY

If psychotherapy has developed as a response to the need for new ways to make sense of human suffering, what factors have contributed to the tremendous growth of psychotherapy in the last half of this century? Researchers Veroff, Kulka, and Douvan, who studied patterns of help seeking on the part of a random sample of Americans between 1957 and 1976, concluded that growing affluence, mobility, and communication and the growth of the mass media contributed to the turn toward psychotherapy.[47] The ability to focus on internal factors rather than survival, the transitory nature of modern society, allowing one to escape one's definition as a member of a family or community, and the media's ability to provide new images and ideals on which to model oneself all contributed to an individual focus on fulfill-ment and peace of mind. According to their study, less than 30 percent of those seeking professional help for a personal problem in 1957 consulted a mental health source of one type or another (psychologists, psychiatrists, social workers, counselors); 49 per-cent of those who sought professional help in 1976 went to a mental health professional. In gross rates, the use of mental health professionals between 1957 and 1976 more than tripled from 4 percent to 13 percent of the total population. Other statis-tics serve to illustrate the growth of psychotherapy:

- Between 1975 and 1985 the number of psychiatrists in-creased by 46 percent (from 26,000 to 38,000), the number of clinical psychologists increased 120 percent (from 15,000 to 33,000), and the number of clinical social workers grew 140 percent (from 25,000 to an estimated 60,000). Also, by 1985 there were an estimated 28,000 licensed marriage and fam-ily therapists.[48]
- As of 1980 there were about 280,000 professional counsel-ors, as well as over 130,000 paraprofessional counselors working in mental hospitals and clinics.[49]
- The U.S. Bureau of Labor Statistics projects that the em-ployment of clinical psychologists, clinical social workers, and mental health counselors in general (particularly those in private practice) will grow faster than the average for all occupations through the year 2000.[50]

These numbers, of course, do not to justice to the overall thera-peutic environment of the times. For example, millions of vol-umes of self-improvement and other popular psychology books continue to be churned out.

The "co-dependent" or "addictive personality" seems to be particularly in vogue. There are now self-help groups for many dependent personality types, and numerous psychotherapists are making a living leading these groups.[51] These groups seem to be a modern manifestation of the role once played by the guilds and friendly societies of the past in that they "promulgate an ide-ology or values through which members may attain an enhanced sense of personal identity."[52] For example, many self-help groups focused on so-called addictive behaviors present a full-fledged personality profile of what it is to be a particular type of addict. Groups for dependent personalities may be only one manifestation of a larger movement for a new communalism in which persons try to find a sense of purpose or meaning by identifying with a particular group. Robert Bly's "men's movement" may be such an avenue for men who cannot accept either their traditional role or that which they perceive to be implied by modern feminism.[53]

On the other hand, the leaders of the self-help movement in America (in contrast to the earlier guilds) almost always locate the source of virtually any kind of suffering within the self. Either the person has a disease (for example, an addictive personality) and must simply learn to live with it, or he or she experienced some kind of trauma as a child and must therefore return to the "inner child" to find a solution to the problem. The proponents of this view are quick to point out that American families are so dysfunctional that virtually everyone, no matter how well healed and otherwise well functioning, needs to be in "recovery" for something. The list of problems that the self-help movement purports to address is so large (encompassing alcoholism, smoking, child abuse, eating disorders, crime, promiscuity, work stress, gambling, poor budgeting, and religious fanaticism) that one is led to believe that if everyone jumped on the bandwagon, all our personal and social problems would disappear in a metamorphosis of personal reflection.

It is undoubtedly true that many people benefit from the structure and support provided by these groups and that some of the problems the groups seek to address are readily dealt with in a group setting. On the other hand, when everyone is encouraged to see themselves as a victim, the public dialogue concerning America's true victims loses focus. David Rieff has pointed out:

> Such an outbreak of self-pity among the affluent classes as recovery has spawned all but ensures that the real victims in American society—those who will never be affluent enough or have enough free time to work it out with their "inner children"—will not get

the attention that is the necessary first step to any improvement in *their* lives.[54]

The radical therapists of the 1960s and 1970s provided a somewhat more pointed sociological argument than Veroff and associates in describing the growth and social function of psychotherapy.[55] They argued that psychotherapy was essentially a mechanism of social control used by capitalism to mystify people as to the true cause of their problems and to reduce dissent. Psychotherapy is seen as having developed from its "guilds" (psychiatrists, psychoanalysts, and social workers), which seek to divide up the therapeutic pie. They claim that the individualistic psychotherapy commonly practiced in this country is ill suited to meet the real needs of poor people and ethnic minorities.

This last criticism has found much support from researchers interested in making psychotherapy more attractive to underprivileged and ethnic minority populations who have historically made less use of psychotherapy than the white middle class.[56] For example, these researchers point out that the therapeutic value placed upon sharing one's innermost feelings or attitudes about one's family with a complete stranger (the therapist) flies in the face of the cultural norms and real-world experience of many nonmajority Americans. The potential shame involved in telling all about one's family renders insight-oriented psychotherapy useless to many Asian Americans, for whom loyalty to family is of paramount importance. Similarly, many African Americans have a lifetime of experience that tells them not to trust Caucasians. It is little wonder that they make less use of psychotherapists (the vast majority of whom are Caucasian) than do Caucasians. Feminists have also been critical of psychotherapy, arguing that the medical, psychoanalytic, and humanistic approaches to therapy often replicate patriarchal interpersonal relationships, which they believe to be at the root of most emotional difficulties for women. In response, some have attempted to create a "feminist therapy."[57]

Does psychotherapy work? The results are mixed, with certain approaches seeming to work better with some problems than others, but with the modest overall measurable effectiveness of psychotherapy indicating that it is far from an exact science.[58] However, this does not have much relevance to the contrast we ultimately hope to make between psychotherapy and social work. Psychotherapy "works" in the sense that it has become a major social institution that carries the function that was once served by magic and faith. It offers analytic therapies to those no longer willing or able to accept a communal ethos. For those unwilling to go it alone, it offers a myriad of therapies of commitment that allow us to feel a part of a larger whole while still leaving the responsibility for most, if not all, of our difficulties within ourselves.

Perhaps a better question is: For whom does psychotherapy work? The man in the car advertisement would probably be going to the right place if he really was visiting a psychotherapist with the problems he mentioned. On the other hand, to refer the woman in our example to a psychotherapist in order to help her with all of the social problems she faces would be a cruel hoax indeed.

SELF-ESTEEM AS SOCIAL POLICY

Psychotherapy is not the only manifestation of expressive individualism in America. Those who sing its praise are always on the lookout for ways to make their private convictions about human perfectibility public, carrying them even into the realm of public policy. There may be no better example of this than the self-esteem movement, which came into public view in 1986 when the California legislature created the Task Force to Promote Self-Esteem and Personal and Social Responsibility. The founders of this movement argued that the development of self-esteem functions as a powerful "social vaccine" against many social problems.

This idea was met with skepticism and, in some quarters, more than a little derision from people who saw it as just another not-too-well-grounded idea coming from the land of loony schemes, hot tubs, and channeling. Most critics felt that, far from being the beginning of a social movement, the task force would amount to nothing more than a short-lived bad joke. They were wrong. Trudeau, creator of *Doonesbury*, was quick to grasp the significance of the task force.

Doonesbury

The self-esteem movement is here, and it has already gone far beyond the boundaries of the Golden State. Louisiana, Virginia, and Maryland have established their own self-esteem task forces, and at least five other states are considering similar efforts.[59] In August 1990, an eleven-country international organization was formed in Oslo at the first international conference on self-esteem.[60] Teachers in particular have latched onto self-esteem as a panacea to cure all the ills that plague American education. Based on her interviews at twenty schools of education across the country, New York journalist and author Rita Kramer was surprised to find that self-esteem was the "dominant education theory" almost everywhere.[61] There has long been a market for such ideas. From one perspective, the self-esteem movement has simply provided a new legitimacy and a potential market for the profiteers of personal perfection as they continue their never-ending quest to sell more books (and now, the ever more popular videotapes) and to fill more lecture halls and retreat venues.

While the larger movement is interesting in and of itself, the more compelling part of the story for us is the decision to make the promotion of self-esteem a matter of public policy. What kind of thinking would lead both the liberal and conservative political leadership in California to devote nearly $735,000 and considerable effort over four years to such a task, particularly during an era of severe fiscal restraint?

We begin with the thinking of the author of the legislation that created the Task Force on Self-Esteem. John Vasconcellos has served for over twenty-five years in the California State Assembly and has been the chairman of its powerful Ways and Means Committee for over a decade. By his own account, he has also spent much of this time "recovering" from a lack of self-esteem evidently developed in the context of a "constrained, traditional, Catholic family."[62] For many years he has been involved in the human potential movement. In the preface to *The Social Importance of Self-Esteem*, a compilation of research findings created originally for the enlightenment of the task force, Vasconcellos described his growing frustration at the expenditure of public funds on programs that he felt missed the root causes of social problems:

> Year after year, we spend ever-increasing billions of tax dollars to contain destructive behaviors, to compensate for human failures after the fact—more than a billion dollars each year for building prisons and two billion for operating them, as well as substantial sums for programs to address alcoholism, drug abuse, teenage pregnancy, child abuse, welfare dependency, and school dropouts.[63]

He noted that all of these programs focused on containment or remediation and that few attempted prevention or cure.

At the same time, Vasconcellos was attuned to what he considered the "emerging evidence" that self-esteem was a factor "central to these problems" and that the strengthening of self-esteem could be a "social vaccine," which would make people "less vulnerable to problem behaviors."[64] He consulted with his friend, Jack Canfield, a "self-esteem expert" who has created a booming business leading seminars and selling books and videos on the topics of self-esteem and peak performance.[65] They decided that it was time to do something about the neglect of self-esteem.

Vasconcellos introduced legislation to create a task force on self-esteem in 1984. In 1986, after gaining bipartisan support in the legislature and putting forth the idea for the third time, Governor George Deukmejian still remained the one political obstacle left in the way of Vasconcellos' vision. The two men had three "very intense" meetings.[66] Deukmejian was not convinced that the government should get involved in the promotion of self-esteem and felt that any study of the matter would be better left to the university. Vasconcellos's reasoning in convincing Deukmejian was similar to the logic he used to gain Republican support in the legislature:

> Think of it in this way: By spending a few tax dollars, we can collect the information and get it out. If that helps even a few persons appreciate and understand self-esteem and how they can live their lives and raise their kids better, we may have less welfare, crime, violence, and drugs—and that's a very conservative use of taxpayers' money.[67]

To this, the governor reportedly replied, "I've never thought of it that way before." Eventually Deukmejian signed Assembly Bill 3659 into law in September 1986, creating the twenty-five-member Task Force to Promote Self-Esteem and Personal and Social Responsibility, with a three-year life span and a budget of $735,000.

Before considering the fate of the task force, let us examine the nature of the conceptual common ground reached between these men of such different political persuasions, to gain some perspective on this meeting of minds and to understand how their thinking was so hopelessly flawed from the outset. In essence, both Vasconcellos and Deukmejian believed that many, if not most, social problems (child abuse, crime and violence, teenage pregnancy, academic failure, alcohol and drug abuse, and chronic welfare dependency) are largely a reflection of limitations or flaws within something that they conceive of as "the self."

To be sure, they came to this conclusion from different directions. Deukmejian's conservative worldview is fully consistent with this perspective. The laissez-faire attitude of conservatives toward collective responsibility for addressing social problems reflects their underlying belief that social problems, for the most part, are a reflection of individual failure or character flaws. Vasconcellos's path to a focus on the self is less straightforward. It took years of immersion in New Age manifestations of expressive individualism to lead him to view the inner world as the source of social ills.

In essence, the line of thinking to which these men adhere reflects a profound misunderstanding of the differences between what the American sociologist C. Wright Mills referred to as "personal troubles" and "public issues." Mills saw personal troubles as essentially private matters restricted to one's character and ability to affect one's immediate social milieu. Public issues, he believed, transcend the individual's milieu and inner life, involving "the larger structure of social and historical life."[68] In this country, the Left often tries to turn troubles into issues; the Right tries to downplay public issues and turn them into a matter that is related to the self.

The focus on the self is an enduring American tradition that found a new expression in the self-esteem movement. This focus reflects the fact that our leaders continue to lack what Mills called, for want of a better name, the "sociological imagination"—that is, the ability or inclination to grasp the intersections between the social and the personal, between "history and biography."[69] Mills described this special quality of mind as follows:

> [Sociological] imagination is the capacity to shift from one perspective to another—from the political to the psychological; from examination of a single family to comparative assessment of the national budgets of the world; from the theological school to the military establishment; from considerations of an oil industry to studies of contemporary poetry. It is the capacity to range from the most impersonal and remote transformations to the most intimate features of the human self—and to see the relations between the two.[70]

In principle, it is equally possible to mistake private troubles for public issues as it is to err in the opposite direction, but it is an underlying premise of this book that the latter occurs much more often than the former in American society. That is, Americans tend to locate the source of human difficulty within the individual, no matter how intricately related it may be to interpersonal, social, political, and historical contexts. The self-esteem movement is unique only in the rather explicit way that it has enlisted government in a wholesale redefinition of public issues as private troubles.

Is there any basis for this redefinition? The results of the efforts of the California Task Force on Self-Esteem and Personal and Social Responsibility shed much light on this question. Since we are mainly interested in whether there are grounds for faith in the power of self-esteem as a "social vaccine," we will focus on the outcome of the first charge to the task force: to compile research regarding the role of self-esteem as a possible causal factor in six areas: child abuse, crime and violence, alcohol and drug abuse, teenage pregnancy, educational failure, and chronic welfare dependency.[71] To do this, they engaged the help of the University of California, which recruited knowledgeable researchers in these areas to summarize relevant information. The results of the investigations of research on the relationship between self-esteem and the social problems selected for study by the legislature can be found in *The Social Importance of Self-Esteem*, edited by Vasconcellos, the task force chair, Andrew Mecca, and distinguished sociologist Neil Smelser.[72]

Did the researchers find that a lack of self-esteem played a significant role in the genesis of social problems? No. Their "intuitive" sense was not confirmed by the vast body of research brought to bear on the subject.

Many of the researchers enlisted to support the task force initially shared the bias of its founders regarding the potential curative powers of self-esteem. Most of the chapters in *The Social Importance of Self-Esteem* showcase seasoned scholars, caught up in the excitement of the task they were given. But the more they delve into existing research, the more obvious it becomes that their early enthusiasm was misplaced; self-esteem plays a minimal or nonexistent role in the creation of the social problems they had set out to study. More important, all of the research reviews point out the significance of factors other than self-esteem, which are beyond the control of the individual but nevertheless play an important role in contributing to the social problems under consideration by the task force.

In his introductory chapter summarizing the results of the research analyses, Smelser was forced to conclude that "the news most consistently reported . . . is that the associations between self-esteem and its expected consequences are mixed, insignificant, or absent," and further, "if the association between self-esteem and behavior is so often reported to be weak, even less can be said for the causal relationship between the two."[73] In other words, although some stretch of the imagination might lead one to see child abuse, crime and violence, welfare dependency, teenage pregnancy, school failure, and many other social problems as personal troubles, available empirical evidence indicates that they should remain public issues.

The research results did not sway the true believers. The final report of the task force reflects the faith of the majority of its members in self-esteem as a social panacea.[74] In fact, one would be hard pressed to discover from the final report that any research was done whatsoever, given that the findings presented appear nowhere in the main body of the report. Smelser's summary of the research findings are relegated to a "personal statements" addendum to the report. One member of the task force who refused to sign the report, David Shannahoff-Khalsa, concluded that the report failed to provide evidence that self-esteem is not "a by-product" of social ills rather than a cause. Shannahoff-Khalsa felt that "the work of the professors has been ignored, and intentionally so" in an effort to "promote the concept of self-esteem as a gospel for salvation."[75] His rage at the dismissal of the research findings was shared by the *Doonesbury* character Hunk-ra, who, in the comic strip, was "channeled" into the task force hearings to provide some insight from beyond.

Doonesbury

BY GARRY TRUDEAU

The appeal of the focus on the self should not be underestimated. California's new "prevention-oriented" Republican governor, Pete Wilson, not only endorsed the recommendations of the task force but appointed its head, Andrew Mecca, to run his drug- and alcohol-abuse programs. The governor's approach to welfare dependency illustrates his understanding of the message of self-esteem. Jack Canfield's Foundation for Self-Esteem developed a "six-hour video-based training program designed to teach welfare recipients how to remove their personal barriers to success, become gainfully employed and achieve their goals."[76] Over 175,000 welfare recipients are slated to go through this program. Wilson also has proposed cutting all benefits to welfare recipients (most of whom are children) by 10 percent, with an additional 15 percent cut after six months for any able-bodied welfare recipient who remains unemployed.* Presumably this unique combination of policy initiatives is intended to provide welfare mothers (and in a small number of cases, fathers) with the requisite high self-esteem and requisite "get up and go" necessary to compete in a job market that exhibits double-digit unemployment. Thus, they will have to enjoy their enhanced self-esteem on a reduced family budget.

This misguided social policy is one example of how the self-esteem movement serves to divert public debate, scarce public resources, and the minds of the American people away from real solutions to social problems and into a celebration of expressive individualism. This movement does not call upon us to sit down together and make decisions about how to use human and economic resources to create a world in which we can all feel good about living. On the contrary, it sends out the message that we need only to look within ourselves (most profitably with the help of a psychotherapist or a human potential "expert") to find the source of all the commonly acknowledged ills that beset society. Vasconcellos himself is quoted as saying at the 1992 Annual Conference of the Association for Humanistic Psychology that "if this spirit of loving were at the heart of politics, we wouldn't have riots and poverty and hunger."[77]

---

*Wilson's proposition was defeated in the 1992 election by a majority vote.

There is a dark subtext to this message that seldom finds direct expression. Those who suffer most directly the effects of social problems—the poor, the homeless, abused children, the frail aged, and the chronically mentally ill—often have the fewest personal resources at their disposal to allow them, in the words of the psychotherapeutic ego psychologists, to "adapt" by finding a "better environment." For these people, the self-esteem message either falls on deaf ears (if they have some perspective on the social forces contributing to their plight), or it contributes to the generally false hope that merely a change of mind will lift them out of their problems. This false hope harkens back to the promises of magic, religion, faith healing, and the power of positive thinking. It also contributes to the lack of faith in collective approaches to problem solving. Those who do not suffer as directly from social ills (generally middle- and upper-class whites) receive a different message from the self-esteemers. They are told that it is not only acceptable but a sign of good emotional health for them to be preoccupied with matters of self-perfection. Furthermore, the idea that all difficulties originate within the individual helps to mitigate any feelings of guilt or even concern that the more fortunate might have regarding their responsibility to do anything about social problems: "It's not *my* problem!"

Efforts by neoconservatives and members of the human potential movement to enlist government support in distracting us from the powerful nature of our interconnectedness are based, at worst, on mean-spirited motivations and, at best, on ignorance. They redirect resources and energy away from programs and ideas that might make a difference in people's lives into programs that verge on quackery and voodoo. Furthermore, they seek to make the promotion of the dark side of American individualism a matter of public policy.

If there is a potentially unifying and worthy goal to which we can aspire with any hope of seriously addressing the societal problems examined by the Task Force on Self-Esteem and Personal and Social Responsibility, that goal must be to acknowledge the interpersonal and social context of all of these problems. We must cultivate for ourselves and others the sociological imagination Mills described over thirty years ago and with it better distinguish the "personal trouble" from the "public issue." This imagination does not result in an abdication of responsibility for one's actions. On the contrary, such a perspective calls forth an appreciation for one's shared destiny with others and the concomitant personal responsibility for engaging collaboratively in the difficult but rewarding job of shaping the future.

No one knew this fact better than many of the early social workers. Social workers certainly have not been immune to the pull of expressive individualism and have provided more than their share of real-life manifestations of the sociological imagination at work.

CHAPTER THREE

THE EMERGENCE OF SOCIAL WORK AS A PROFESSION

"Is there a doctor in the house?"

Imagine a theater. The manager steps through the closed curtain to ask this question of the audience. All of the members of the audience are likely to assume that someone backstage is ill, and the manager is seeking the help of an expert to deal with the problem.

Now suppose that the manager asked, instead:

"Is there a psychotherapist in the house?"

This might cause the audience some amusement, but people would nonetheless conjure a picture of someone having an emotional crisis for which the manager was seeking professional assistance.

But what if the manager asked:

"Is there a social worker in the house?"

Chances are that the members of the audience would have very different thoughts about the sort of problem the manager was trying to deal with. One reason for this response is that the public lacks a clear sense of the kind of expertise a professional social worker has. This lack of clarity occurs because the profession itself is unclear about its social mission and uncertain about the practice methodology that is best suited to carry out one or another mission.

This chapter and the two that follow describe the emergence of social work as a profession. This historical review explains how the profession evolved from systems of patronage, piety, Elizabethan Poor Law, and charity and philanthropy and how it began early in this century to merge with the practice of psychotherapy.

Professions are the means by which people specialize in carrying out tasks that in an earlier day were performed by the family in an extended kinship group and by members of the tribe or village. The first specialists to emerge in less-developed societies were the medicine man, the priest, and the shaman.

Historically, it fell to members of the family or others in the tribe or village to care for orphaned children, the frail aged, and the disabled, retarded, and mentally ill. Feudalistic society was relatively well structured and stable. It was highly stratified and hierarchical, and all members of it, ranging from the lord of the manor down to the villein, had explicit rights and responsibilities that were appropriate to their different statuses.

Industrialization has been the great motor of social and economic change in our era. With industrialization and the breakup of the feudal system, social and economic life became less stable. In industrial society, relationships are based less on status (on a position in life that has permanency and stability) and more on contract (particular arrangements made for particular economic and social exchanges).[1] There were, too, in industrial society, higher degrees of specialization. Professionalization of functions is a manifestation of specialization.

The oldest and the most prestigious professions in Western society are the ministry, law, university teaching, and medicine. Social work, library science, education, and nursing are relative newcomers to the professional legions. As such, they are both less well developed and less prestigious, and they have less status in society than the older professions. Some scholars refer to social work and these other relative newcomers as "semiprofessions" because their professional attributes are not yet fully developed.[2]

ANTECEDENTS: PATRONAGE, PIETY, POOR LAW, AND PHILANTHROPY

The modern profession of social work is based on large elements of patronage, piety, Poor Law, and philanthropy, all different arrangements for dealing with social problems that developed after the breakup of feudal society but preceding twentieth-century social work.[3]

Patronage

The patron-client relationship is based on an ancient system of social exchange that predates the almsgiving of the church and the system of social control instituted by English Poor Law. This relationship continues to operate fully and effectively in many societies even today. The *patrocinium* of ancient Rome have their present-day counterparts in the *mafiosi* of Sicily. The *caciques* of Spain, the *mugata'ji* of Lebanon, the *oyabun* of Japan, and the *caudillos* of Colombia are other contemporary examples of the patronage system.[4]

The patron is a middleman, a pivotal figure who is positioned to deal with two kinds of clients: members of society's social and economic elites and the upwardly mobile, ambitious, aggressive, and frequently troublesome members of society's lower class. Although they are not usually illegal, patronage systems are often viewed as somewhat disreputable and not quite legitimate, probably because patronage transactions involve members of the lower social classes. To put the matter bluntly, the patron's function is to control the movement of some members of lower social and economic classes into higher classes. The patron selects the members of the lower class who are most likely to succeed as members of the higher classes. These are people who will be most appealing to and acceptable to members of the privileged classes for various reasons: because they are the right color, for example, or have the right accent, manner, or intellectual, artistic, or technical abilities.

Until about the middle of this century, American society had a well-developed system of political patronage in most cities, called the boss system.[5] It generally faded with the professionalization of many of the functions of political bosses and ward heelers and their appointees. These functions, which included getting people jobs, giving them financial support, and helping them with legal problems, are now for the most part carried out by professionals—usually social workers—who work in public services, are selected through bureaucratically controlled civil service systems, and are advanced through equally bureaucratic merit systems.

Most recently, the best examples of the patronage system in American society are the private foundations, a significant institution. With capital holdings of approximately $122 billion in 1990, 30,338 foundations distributed approximately $7.4 billion annually for various cultural, educational, health, and social purposes.[6] Professionals who work for foundations carry out the patronage function for their wealthy employers by managing the introduction of new social, cultural, political, and economic ideas into society. Essentially, foundation professionals search out and screen new leadership from disenfranchised groups, such as minority populations, unknown and developing artists, and unrecognized intellectuals in order to introduce them to "respectable" society.

In some respects, social workers are still in the business of providing patronage to the lower classes. For example, advocacy and brokerage are considered to be important social work functions in which professionals represent their clients' interests in dealing with organizations and institutions.[7] In some kinds of community organization and community development (a social work specialization), the social work professional helps service users to improve their position in dealing with social and political elites.[8] This occurs, for example, in programs in which tenants are organized to negotiate with landlords for better housing conditions and welfare clients are organized to demand increased benefits and better services from welfare departments.

Piety

Piety is another strong historical element in social work. The church was the first institution to pick up the functions of communal support for the poor after the breakup of the feudal estates. The poor (in the Middle Ages, the majority of the population) were cared for by the clergy with financial support from the nobility.[9] Their major motivation was service to God. Charity was believed to be an act of piety, one of the good works that ensured the pious a place in heaven. The church carried out this function for a couple of centuries.

In contemporary society there continues to be a religious base of social service. Jewish philanthropies and Catholic charities, for example, continue to serve many communities. Thousands of church organizations provide charitable services to poor and deprived people in both the United States and abroad. Thus, there continue to be large elements of piety and religiosity in social work and social welfare.

Piety, however, has become an embarrassment to all professions, including many members of the clergy. The idea of a professional's being committed to such values as morality, virtue, community good, and altruism is considered by many to be maudlin and intellectually unsophisticated. Today many people support government and service organizations that are more interested in hard numbers, efficiency, and economy than in protecting children and caring for dependent people.

Poor Law

The system of income supports in the United States (which is known as public assistance and social security but is sometimes called relief or welfare) has its origins in the Elizabethan Poor Laws, promulgated in 1601 by Elizabeth I to deal with the provision of income supports for paupers.[10] Previously, English laws for dealing with the poor had been, for the most part, repressive labor legislation; for example, the intent of laws like the Statute of Artificers and the Act of 1531 was to control the movements of laborers and to prevent them from organizing in any way to make demands on their employers.[11] With the Poor Laws, Elizabeth laid upon each county the responsibility of caring for poor persons who had their origins in that county. These laws were based on the belief that locality of origin should be the source of help for people in time of need.

The American colonists transposed the Elizabethan Poor Laws to the American mainland, establishing the major patterns of relief giving in the United States until the passage of the Social Security Act of 1935. But even today, some values from the Elizabethan Poor Laws persist in our welfare system. For example, the law of settlement is the basis for the notion of local responsibility for the poor. Counties throughout the United States continue to transport people who are eligible for general assistance back to their counties of origin. "Less eligibility" is another English Poor Law idea that has persisted to the present. This refers to the practice of providing income supports to eligible recipients at levels below what is established as their real need, on the principle that the benefits received by welfare recipients should be noticeably less than the salaries of the lowest-paid workers. In the United States today, no state pays income support benefits to dependent children and general assistance recipients that are up to the level of need that the states themselves establish.

The values of Elizabethan Poor Law are the basis of the least flattering view of social work. In this view, social work represents middle-class morality framed as a profession and serves a regulatory function with respect to the lower classes; social workers are gatekeepers to services and benefits needed by the poor.

In the early American Republic, poor people, dependent children, the mentally ill, and the frail aged were frequently dealt with together in the county jail or in lunatic asylums, the workhouse, or the poorhouse. Not until the mid-nineteenth century was any systematic thought given to sorting out the different needs of people who turned for help to charities and the county programs.

In the 1850s, as the result of a movement for reform spearheaded by Dorothea Dix, the states developed hospitals in which to treat the mentally ill. In 1854, President Franklin Pierce vetoed a bill under which federal lands could have been used by the states to establish mental hospitals; Pierce believed that the responsibility to provide care for the mentally ill fell on the states, not the federal government.[12] It would be more than a century before the federal government would agree to assume any responsibility to assist the states in providing adequate care for this population.

Poor Law values continue to pervade our system of public assistance and public social services, despite the fact that a large proportion of the American middle class receives income supports—social security, farm subsidies, loans for education, in-

come tax deductions for home mortgages and for costs of medical care, and tax subsidies for retirement incomes—from the programs of what Neil Gilbert and Barbara Gilbert refer to as "the
Enabling State." The programs for the poor that constitute the
Reagan/Bush safety net—school lunches, Aid to Families with
Dependent Children, and the general assistance programs of the
states and counties—are small by comparison to the programs
for the middle class provided by the enabling state.[13] Nonetheless, programs for the poor, and especially programs for poor
children and young parents, continue to be given support only
grudgingly. They are both means tested and mean spirited, and
most are deliberately made unattractive. Social workers employed in public social services agencies work under unpleasant
and sometimes dangerous conditions, as they have in the past.
Over one hundred years ago, Charles Loring Brace, director of
the Society for the Prevention of Pauperism, referred to work
with "the dangerous classes": "the ignorant, destitute, untrained,
and abandoned youth: the outcaste street children—grown up to
be voters, to be the implements of demagogues, the 'feeders' of
the criminals, and the sources of domestic outbreaks and violations of the law."[14]

Today, social workers who choose to make their careers in the
public services are familiar with the potential dangers. They receive little support and encouragement from their community,
their profession, and political leaders. Thus, it is no surprise that
many social workers choose not to make their careers in the public social services, and many who do begin their careers in the
public sector become burned out by the hard work and lack of
support.

Many social workers find it difficult to deal with one other aspect of the public social services: they are often expected to carry
out the state's social control functions with respect to the protection of children and certain dependent adults. As a result, frequently they are put in the position of having to represent the
interests of the courts and law enforcement agencies—a task that
many find to be undesirable, in part because it conflicts with the
helping and enabling function. For example, many social workers deal with parents who are accused of neglecting and abusing
their children. Presumably the social worker's objective is to help

parents carry out their child-rearing responsibilities more effectively. If there is an increase in abusive behavior at some point, the social worker may decide that it is in a child's best interests to have him or her removed from the parents' home. The parent may then accuse the worker of being duplicitous. (Some jurisdictions have dealt with this problem by vesting the child-protective functions and the parent-helping functions in two different workers. However, this separation of functions may increase considerably the costs of services.)

Additionally social workers find the social control function to be unattractive because it is associated with law enforcement, and the personnel who work for the police and for probation and parole are usually more likely to be of working-class origins than other professionals. Thus, from the point of view of prestige and status, the social work professional is more likely to reject the social control functions of social care and embrace the clinical function.

Philanthropy

In the eighteenth and nineteenth centuries, the landed gentry who benefited from the Acts of Enclosure and the successful industrialists were able to amass great fortunes, and some of these wealthy people established private charities whose function it was to provide relief to the poor. By the end of the nineteenth century, there were hundreds of such charities in all large American cities. They were usually run by individuals and families, each in its own way.

The systems of giving through charities were haphazard. Lacking any systematic criteria for determining need, sponsors of the charities gave for their own purposes—sometimes to provide relief and succor to the needy but just as often to strengthen the spiritual and moral fiber of the recipient.

In the latter part of the nineteenth century, only 20 percent of the United States population was urban and 80 percent was rural—about the reverse of what it is today. Most American cities had their major growth during and after the Civil War, so there was no reservoir of political and professional experience on which to draw in dealing with urban problems. The fact that we are doing so poorly in dealing with similar problems a century later suggests that this kind of knowledge and wisdom develops very slowly.

In the nineteenth century, charitable relief was given in various forms (e.g., money, a food basket, a cord of wood). However, private charities were often more flexible and generous than local governments in providing public relief. Frequently, public aid was given as indoor relief: recipients had to reside in the workhouse or the poorhouse.

One must reach into the American past to study American poorhouses; the last systematic analysis of them from a contemporary view was written in the 1890s by Amos Warner, who documented the ways in which the different states were phasing out the almshouses: "The almshouse is the fundamental institution in American poor relief. . . . It is ordinarily a depressing experience to visit an almshouse, and accordingly we find it an institution that even the benevolent willingly forget." He recognized also that a sure way to train paupers was to rear children in almshouses.[15] Poorhouses remained a part of the American scene for some time. During the Great Depression, they sprang up throughout the nation as a means of dealing with poverty. They were always considered a stigma and associated with humiliation, as Will Carleton captured in his poem, "Over the Hill to the Poorhouse," which we quote here:

> Over the hill to the poor-house I'm
> . trudgin' my weary way—
> I, a woman of seventy, and only a trifle
> gray—
> I, who am smart an' chipper, for all
> the years I've told,
> As many another woman that's only
> half as old.
>
> What is the use of heapin' on me a
> pauper's shame?
> Am I lazy or crazy? am I blind or
> lame?
> True, I am not so supple, nor yet so
> awful stout;
> But charity ain't no favor, if one can
> live without.

Over the hill to the poor-house—
  my child'rn dear, goodby!
Many a night I've watched you when
  only God was nigh;
And God'll judge between us; but I will
  al'ays pray
That you shall never suffer the half I
  do today.[16]

Private philanthropies frequently were a desirable alternative to public relief for poor people. They assumed the major responsibility for relief giving, especially in the cities, up until the 1930s, when they and the states themselves were overwhelmed by the extent of economic need.

With the passage of the Social Security Act of 1935, when the federal government assumed a major part of the responsibility for income-support programs for the poor, the functions of the private charities changed. No longer called upon to provide alms for the poor, they went into the business of providing social services, primarily social casework of a psychotherapeutic nature.[17] This division occurred neither unconsciously nor accidentally. Gordon Hamilton, who was among the most influential of social caseworkers in the country from the 1930s to the 1950s, laid out the agenda as early as 1931: "Generally speaking, as family maintenance cases, mother's aid, etc., are taken over by public welfare agencies . . . the private societies will tend to take cases where the interest attaches to the unadjusted personality rather than to economic factors."[18]

Philanthropy, or what is today called the private/voluntary sector, has developed in diverse ways. First, the private, philanthropic/voluntary agencies (e.g., Family Service Association, United Way, and Urban League) constitute a small but significant part of social welfare. However, it is estimated that currently approximately 50 percent of the budgets of these agencies comes from public funds.[19] Governmental support of voluntary programs occurs through third-party contracts and subventions. Thus, voluntary agencies are frequently not quite as voluntary as may appear at first glance. The result of these arrangements is that voluntary/private welfare organizations are hardly distinguishable from public organizations.

Second, there has been extensive growth of employer-provided social services (usually referred to as employee assistance programs) consisting primarily of treatment for drug and alcohol dependency and, less frequently, of benefits counseling, psychotherapy, child care, and elder care. Professionals who operate these programs come primarily from psychology and to a lesser (but growing) extent from social work.

Employee assistance programs provide services for a working population and cover a wide range of social class groups. More important, their raison d'être is to serve the interests of the (usually profit-making) organizations that employ them. Certainly, these services are of some benefit to the employees that make use of them. Ultimately, though, the service must be beneficial to the industry that pays for it. Questions about whether these services are the best means for helping individuals and whether they are good for the community cannot be of foremost concern to professionals operating these programs.

Finally, a significant proportion of social workers are now in private for-profit practice, either individually or working for profit-making organizations.

The profession of social work emerged in the twentieth century with a legacy of an ancient system of social welfare, based on the four elements of patronage, piety, Poor Law, and philanthropy. Remnants of each of these elements can be found in social work practice today, yet many social workers find this legacy unattractive. Emerging from the nineteenth century with qualities that many of today's professionals find undesirable, social work is a two-tiered profession: publicly supported, means-tested, underfunded, poorly staffed programs for the poor and vested programs such as social security for the middle class (often referred to as the entitlement programs, suggesting that the claims of recipients of these benefits are of greater legitimacy than the claims of recipients of the safety-net programs). In addition, the middle class is offered the clinical programs of pure psychotherapy or of psychotherapeutically oriented services, often purchased on a private basis through insurance or paid for directly by the person, or the employer, or by a public agency.

To say that poor people receive only means-tested, nonclinical, and poorly staffed services and benefits and that middle-class people receive only entitlement kinds of benefits and highly professional and psychotherapeutically based services is exaggerated, but generally that is the case.

THE CHARITIES AND THE SETTLEMENTS

The latter half of the nineteenth century and the years leading up to World War I were filled with social movements pressing for recognition of the social, political, and economic rights of the working man (and, later, the working woman). Abolitionism, Christian temperance, trade unionism, charities and corrections, sexual hygiene, and planned parenthood were some of the significant social movements of the era. Two social movements in social welfare that began in the last quarter of the nineteenth century affected the development of the profession of social work: the Charity Organization Societies (COS) and the settlement houses.[20] Both movements originated in England and both were part of the larger charities and corrections movement.

Charities and Corrections Movement

The charities and corrections movement came about as an effort to rationalize charitable giving in American communities. In 1865, Massachusetts was the first state to appoint a Board of Public Charities. This board, in turn, organized the Social Science League, which held the first national meeting on charities in 1865 and led to the founding of the American Social Science Association. By 1874, nine states had boards of charities, and they organized the National Conference on Charities and Corrections.

The charities and corrections movement was based on a powerful belief in the perfectibility of society—a belief that has dwindled and atrophied over the course of a century. It is difficult today to envision the passion and fervor of that movement. The charities and corrections people were concerned about every corner of darkness, despair, and deprivation on earth: the "feeble-minded," the insane, criminals, drunks, the tubercular, epileptics, pure food and drugs, the poor, children, sanitation, play-grounds, disaster relief, and so forth. Many of the reforms they sought—the forty-hour work week, social security, child labor laws, and disaster relief—have become institutionalized during this century, and we now take them for granted, but in the nineteenth century, these ideas were considered radical.

The charities and corrections people were ruled by a fierce Victorian morality, and they were determined to uplift every fallen sparrow they came upon. Darwinism, eugenics, and social mechanics were their intellectual tools. The major ideas of the charities and corrections movement came from philosophers like Herbert Spencer; physicians like Benjamin Rush, Emil Kraepelin, and Adolf Meyer; and political scientists like J. Allen Smith and Robert M. La Follette. They believed that human fortunes are determined largely by physical and biological forces, which a benevolent and enlightened upper class can control through social engineering and use of new intellectual tools from the developing sciences of eugenics, sociology, anthropology, and psychology. These sciences, like industry of the day, were preoccupied with mechanics. Their moral beliefs were based on the relatively fixed social class structure of the time; the principle of noblesse oblige—that the upper classes were responsible for helping the poor—prevailed.

The pages of the *Proceedings of the Conference of Charities and Corrections* are filled with papers presenting carefully assembled statistics on charities and public welfare analyses of social problems, such as homeless newsboys, immigration, tuberculosis, and unsanitary living conditions and sermonizing about the evils of the dance halls, the five-cent theater, liquor, poolrooms, and candy stores. Following is an excerpt from a 1914 paper on the bad influences of the candy store:

> The great objections to the candy store as found at present are three-fold: it destroys morals and health, and develops bad habits. By candy stores we do not mean the ordinary grocery store where parents come and go, where the grocer makes part of his profit from the sale of groceries, where the moral tone of the place is kept up by the presence of the parents, but we refer to the little shop

where sweets are sold and where children gather merely to spend their time for lack of something else to do. During the cooler evenings of the spring, fall and winter, both sexes, little boys and little girls, gather in these centers which sometimes keep open as late as the saloon. In the pool room we have only young men, in the saloon men, but in the candy store and other like centers, where children gather, we allow both sexes to associate without any supervision of the places which harbor them. The things sold in the store which the children eat are frequently injurious to health. The study of some two hundred children, largely newsboys, showed that nearly one-third had chronic indigestion. Irregular eating, and eating of harmful food and sweets, means that by the time our children have reached the age of twenty-five to thirty they will be wrecked physically. Digestive organs are injured beyond repair. Again the candy store promotes physical inactivity—sitting, which means that the muscles and organs of the body cannot be normally developed. . . .

The candy store develops habits of thriftlessness and a desire to spend money for foolish, worthless things. A glance at the things in the windows shows hardly anything of value, unless it be some sporting goods, but mostly such articles as will tempt the children to spend their pennies. We have not realized the part the candy store plays in furnishing patrons for the saloons, but you will find upon careful study that the habits, the tastes, the desires, which are cultivated by the candy store and like social centers naturally assert themselves and seek satisfaction as the child grows too old to make the candy store his hangout.[21]

By the standards of the early charity workers, today's MTV generation would be considered a clearly lost cause.

Charity Organization Societies and Mary E. Richmond

The Conference on Charities and Corrections took an important turn in the direction of a focused interest in the development of practice with the rise of the Charity Organization Societies (COS). The Reverend Humphries Gurteen established the first COS in the United States in Buffalo in 1877. Gurteen's announcement of the principles of the COS are not unlike some contemporary views of social welfare:

The basic axiom, the cardinal principle of the "Charity Organization Society" is diametrically opposed to all systems, all institutions, all charities, all forms of relief whatsoever, which avowedly or tacitly adopt the creed of Charles Lamb to "give and ask no questions," or which is worse, that system of injudicious questioning at the door or on the street, which leads the beggar on to invent additional falsehoods. The fundamental law of its operation is expressed in one word, "*Investigate.*" Its motto is: "No relief (except in extreme cases of despair or imminent death) without previous and searching examination." It says virtually to the distributors of official relief, "refrain from giving a single cent until the individual case of each applicant has been thoroughly examined." Its axiom, accordingly, is, *"Help the poor to help themselves."*[22]

Currently, the nearest equivalent we have of the COS is the United Way but only with respect to the fact that both organizations are concerned with the coordination of philanthropic resources. (Actually, the Community Chest movement of the early twentieth century replaced the COS. The Community Chest movement evolved into the United Way, and the COS became the Family Service Association of America, an organization that continues to operate in American cities.) The primary functions of the COS were the elimination of "indiscriminate giving" and the "repression of mendicancy." The COSs did not themselves give charity to applicants. Rather, they screened applicants for the charities; those found to be worthy of assistance were referred to an appropriate charity. Thus, the COS served as a central registry, which was a way of ensuring that supplicants for charity were not double dipping.

The COS was a significant innovation in social work and social welfare; it represented the first institutional effort to go about the business of dealing with poor people in a systematic way. COS workers practiced what was called "scientific charity" (though the word *rational* would have been a better way to describe what they actually did because there was very little science involved). Scientific charity consisted of a social investigation of applicants to discover what resources they might have available to them and the assignment of a "friendly visitor," a COS volunteer who advised the recipient. Hence the motto of the COS was, "Not alms, but a friend!" The COS sought to "send each family a persevering faithful friend, who, by . . . personal influence will . . . teach them habits of industry and self-control."[23] Over the next fifty years, the scientific investigation evolved into the clinical interview; the faithful friend turned into, first, the social caseworker and, later, the psychotherapist; and the personal influence came to be exercised through a therapeutic relationship.

There is not much of a record of just what the early friendly visitors did in their encounters with their subjects, although they seem to have moralized to, coached, and instructed the visitees. Writing about the practice of friendly visiting in 1887, Marian C. Putnam said that "the low standard of morality and intelligence, and the lack of self-control, that keeps large numbers of people very poor and degraded, come partly from external conditions that may be improved, and partly from weak wills that may be strengthened and wrong tendencies that may be checked."[24] Morals were often considered the most important of the elements. In 1895, Linda Richards, a charity organizationist who worked for the placement of trained nurses in hospitals, wrote pridefully: "No word of profanity is ever heard in a hospital where trained nurses are found!"[25] Most of the friendly visitors were volunteers, and most of them were middle- and upper-class women. The executive secretary of the COS was usually a paid employee.

Mary Ellen Richmond, a gifted woman who established early in this century the basic principles of social casework practice, began her career with the Charity Organization Society of Baltimore in 1888. Her life, more than any other, illustrates the development of a profession that would, for a century, search for a method. Although she did not intend it, she prepared the profession for its warm embrace of psychiatry, psychoanalysis, and psychotherapy.

Richmond was born in 1861 and was orphaned at an early age. Raised by relatives who had limited financial means, she received little formal education beyond high school. She was, though, an avid reader, and, it appears she was trained early in life to put in writing her views about what she had read.[26]

Her young adult years were a time of struggle; she supported herself despite problems of ill health and also carrying the burden of caring for an invalid aunt. In 1888, Richmond responded to a newspaper advertisement for a position as assistant treasurer of the Charity Organization Society of Baltimore, at a salary of fifty dollars a month.[27] The leadership of the Baltimore COS, established in 1881, represented some of the bluest blood of the eastern seaboard: Daniel Coit Gilman (president of the Johns Hopkins University), John Glenn, Charles J. Bonaparte, and Amos G. Warner.

Richmond shaped the business of friendly visiting into the professional practice of social work.[28] Very early, she began to lay out the process of doing a social investigation of applicants for charity that she called a "social diagnosis." One of her earliest efforts to present this material is a paper she read at the National Conference on Charities and Corrections in 1901, "Charitable Co-operation," in which she described the process of "helping the person in his situation."[29] She conceived of the task of making a social diagnosis in a way that today we can describe as social systems theory, that is, that all social units—individuals, groups, organizations, communities—are systems subject to the same rules of behavior. Any system has an internal organization of subsystems and is related to other systems in its environment. For example, an individual may be conceived of as a system made up of various physical and emotional subsystems. The individual is related to other individual systems and is a subsystem of larger systems, such as the family, the social group, and the occupational group. A social group can be viewed as a system of individuals and subgroups that constitute its subsystems, and the social group is a subsystem of a larger system, such as an organization or the community.[30] (See figure 1.)

Mary Richmond had this conception of practice at a time when there had not yet been articulated anything like social systems theory, when there was no profession as such to which to relate these ideas, and when there was not a social services system of any kind to which to connect these formulations. Even more significant, Richmond thought that an important part of the process of solving the problem lay in understanding the person and his or her situation. This may not seem like much of an insight from the perspective of the 1990s, when, behavioral analysis is one of the favorite indoor sports of all social classes. But at the beginning of this century, very few Americans had even heard the name of Sigmund Freud. People were generally less introspec-

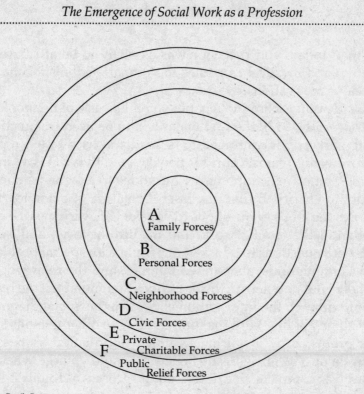

A.—*Family Forces.*
    Capacity of each member for
      Affection.
      Training.
      Endeavor.
      Social development.

B.—*Personal Forces.*
    Kindred.
    Friends.

C.—*Neighborhood Forces.*
    Neighbors, landlords, tradesmen.
    Former and present employers.
    Clergymen, Sunday-school teacers, fellow
      church member.s
    Doctors.
    Trade-unions, fraternal and benefit societies,
      social clubs, fellow-workmen.
    Libraries, educational clubs, classes,
      settlements, etc.
    Thrift agencies, savings-banks, stamp-savings,
      building and loan associations.

D.—*Civic Forces.*
    School-teachers, truant officers.
    Police, police magistrates, probation officers,
      reformatories.

Health department, sanitary inspectors, factory
    inspectors.
Postmen.
Parks, baths, etc.

E.—*Private Charitable Forces.*
    Charity organization society.
    Church of demonation to which family belongs.
    Benevolent individuals.
    National, special, and general relief societies.
    Charitable employment agencies and work-
      rooms.
    Fresh-air society, children's aid society, society
      for protection of children, children's homes,
      etc.
    District nurses, sick-diet kitchens, dispensaries,
      hospitals, etc.
    Society for suppression of vice, prisoner's aid
      society, etc.

F.—*Public Relief Forces.*
    Almshouses.
    Outdoor poor department.
    Public hospitals and dispensaries.

Figure 1 *Mary Richmond's "Diagram of Forces with Which the Charity Worker May Co-operate"*

tive than today, and behavior was as likely to be attributed to
spiritual and mystical causes as to rational, hedonistic, and unconscious motivations.

The ideas in Richmond's paper were the basis of her book, *Social Diagnosis* (1917), the first major text to be used by practicing
social workers.[31] It continued to be read and used to teach practice for twenty years. A curious book to read today, it is a kind of
catalog and classification of the questions to ask the person applying for charity. It first discusses the nature of evidence, then
explores the kinds of questions to be asked of everyone (the com-
position of the family, work, and medical history), and finally
deals with questions to be asked of people with special problems,
such as immigrants, abandoned families, and the retarded, and
alcoholic. But nowhere in the book does Richmond tell the reader
what to do with the information elicited in this social diagnosis.
She had an abiding faith that one could help other persons solve
their problems by acquiring as much information as possible
about them. The answer, she believed, would emerge when the
record was complete. She described the process as follows:

> Social diagnosis is the attempt to arrive at as exact a definition as
> possible of the social situation and personality of a given client.
> The gathering of evidence, or investigation, begins the process,
> the critical examination and comparison of evidence follows, and
> last come its interpretation and the definition of the social diffi-
> culty. Where one word must describe the whole process, *diagnosis*
> is a better word than *investigation*, though in strict use the former
> belongs to the end of the process.[32]

Richmond recorded many of her interviews with applicants
and, later, when she went to work as director of the Department
of Social Work at the Russell Sage Foundation in New York City,
copies of her records and the forms she used for agency intake
were purchased by social workers all over the country for use in
teaching. As a result of her dedication to the writing of what were
called process records, generations of social workers wrote an
endless number of lengthy records, most of them useless, for
their supervisors.

If *Social Diagnosis* provided so little in the way of practical intervention to solve problems, why was the book of such great in-

terest to professionals of that day? The reason was that up to that time it had not occurred to the people who dealt with paupers and other dependent persons that anything of value could be learned by talking to them. The upper classes were confident that they understood the causes of dependency: belief in eugenics and the heritability of such traits as alcoholism, indolence, and intelligence remained strong in social work well into the 1930s; theories of racial inferiority were held in respect to immigrants; the essential superiority and moral rightness of the upper classes were assumed. Mary Richmond opened a new world of inquiry to friendly visitors and social investigators. Her book provided them with a compendium of pertinent questions to put to applicants, and her intake forms and process recordings were means of storing the information.

Richmond devoted her life during the first quarter of this century to the development of social casework. She lectured extensively, was instrumental in the development of social work education programs, and consulted continuously with COSs throughout the United States. Prior to World War I, she was the preeminent social worker in the United States, both because of her position at the Russell Sage Foundation and because of the success of her book.

After the United States entered World War I, Richmond was called upon by the Red Cross to establish the Home Service. Social work in general developed considerably as a result of World War I. Both psychiatric social work and Richmond's brand of social treatment were offered on a large scale to servicemen, their families, and veterans. Richmond herself selected the name "Home Service" for this program, which provided services (e.g., arranging for income maintenance, hospital discharge, and relocation) to soldiers and sailors in France and to their families at home. By June 1918 there were 3,400 Home Service sections in the United States staffed by 40,000 workers, most of them volunteers.[33]

Although the Home Service had the potential of developing into a national system of social services, the Red Cross lost interest in supporting it after the war, and Richmond herself was unenthusiastic about programs supported by any large organization, public or private. The Home Service was completely disbanded in 1921.[34] However, psychiatric social work continued to flourish, becoming a major practice in the U.S. Public Health Service hospitals and the Veterans Bureau.

Richmond was probably not entirely satisfied with how she saw the field developing in the 1920s. She was uneasy about the profession's enthusiastic rush to associate itself with and to use psychiatry and psychoanalysis as its major methods, and she seemed to be uneasy about the utility of social diagnosis. She wrote in 1920 that, after the social investigation, "the treatment seems to drop to a lower level as though it went over a cliff." That is, there was no clear line of practice to follow after the social diagnosis was completed. Richmond's expectation that complete information about a person's problem would lead to its solution was not realized.[35]

Richmond had read Freud and Jung but was dubious about psychiatry's being the theory of choice for social work. She thought, though, that there was much promise in small-group psychology. What was needed, she said, were "expert observations of the normal reactions of two or more persons to one another. . . . Halfway between individual psychology and studies of neighborhoods . . . there is a field almost as yet unexplored." And, she added sadly, "I have neither the time nor the equipment for such an excursion."[36] She was, of course, reaching for a set of theories that we today call social psychology, but that set of theories did not begin to crystallize until the 1940s—too late for Richmond and too late for social work. In the absence of better theory, Richmond was drawn inexorably to conclude that the central aim of social casework was the "maintenance and development of personality."[37]

The Settlement House Movement and Jane Addams

The settlement house movement began in England in the late 1800s with the establishment of Toynbee Hall in London's East End by some young graduates of Oxford University. The idea behind the settlements was for middle- and upper-class young men and women to establish residence—to settle and live—in working-class neighborhoods. The settlement house represented a voluntary renunciation of privilege and position; it was an expression of a strong desire to be of service to the poor. These liberal-minded and well-educated young men and women believed that by participating in the life of the neighborhood, they would raise the cultural, moral, and intellectual level of the community.

The settlements provided child care for working mothers, health clinics, and classes in dance, arts, culture, and domestic sciences. The relatively intimate relationships that developed among all the participants led the settlers to come to appreciate the rich social and cultural life of working-class communities.

Jane Addams, a contemporary of Mary Richmond, was the best-known leader of the settlement house movement in the United States. Born in 1860 of an upper-middle-class family, she became a legend in her own time. Her father, a miller and successful businessman, was a personal friend of Abraham Lincoln. Although a Quaker, he supported the Union in the Civil War, recruiting and outfitting his own regiment, the Addams Guard.

By the turn of the century, Addams was the most famous woman in America. In 1931, she was awarded (with Nicholas Butler, president of Columbia University) the Nobel Prize, the only social worker ever to receive one. (The prize was given to her for her efforts for peace, not for her accomplishments in social work.) Addams, an ardent feminist, donated the prize money to the Women's League for Peace and Freedom, which she had helped found.

Addams had a fine formal education. She attended the Rockford Female Seminary and graduated at the head of her class in 1881. She began studies at Women's Medical College but dropped out after one year because of poor health. As a student, she took an interest in social and political issues.

Addams suffered some bouts of illness while young. Both to recuperate and to keep herself occupied, she traveled abroad several times. On one of these trips, she visited the settlement houses in England and was deeply impressed with the work they did. She returned to the United States eager to undertake a similar project.

In 1889, using her own money, she and another young woman rented a building in Chicago that became Hull House, the best-known settlement house in the United States. This was an unusual and imaginative course of action for young women at that time and, in the eyes of many Americans, an adventurous and ennobling social experiment. Outside of teaching school or serving as a governess, there was little for an upper-middle-class woman to do if she did not marry and become a homemaker. Addams threw herself into settlement house work, recruiting residents, raising funds, developing a program, and engaging in social action and politics.

They began their work at Hull House by letting their neighbors know they were "at home" to them. Hull House was in the heart of a crowded working-class neighborhood filled with immigrants from Greece, Italy, and Germany. They started with readings and discussions and showing slides of Florentine art. The neighbors came—some from curiosity, others for the opportunity for some relief and diversion from their own crowded and poor homes. By 1893, there were some forty clubs and other activities including a day nursery, gymnasium, dispensary, and playground. Later they added an art gallery, a little theater, and a music school.

The settlers at Hull House associated themselves with many social reform movements; they were defenders of organized labor, they supported such causes as the outlawing of child labor, and they fought for women's suffrage. In the first years of Hull House, Addams nearly succeeded in unseating a powerful city councilman. Her social action and political activities captured a good deal of public attention and ignited the imagination of people all over the world. Hull House and the young women who had set out on this extraordinary program were written about extensively, and Addams came to be admired as a saintlike figure. She began to receive significant recognition early in her career. In 1910, she became the first woman to receive an honorary degree from Yale University. In 1911 she became head of the National Federation of Settlements, a post she held for life.

Addams had an outstanding ability to recruit people and to work with them, and she brought an extraordinary collection of people to the settlement: Florence Kelly, Sophonisba Breckenridge, John Dewey, William James, Governor John Peter Altgeld, Clarence Darrow, the historian Charles Beard, Edith and Grace

Abbot, Julia Lathrop, James Ruskin, Sidney and Beatrice Webb, and William Morris.[38]

Addams succeeded in bringing to the attention of the emerging profession of social work a perspective on practice that was very different from the thrust of Mary Richmond's work. Settlement house workers had an appreciation of the importance of helping immigrants to maintain their cultural and family ties. Addams helped the field to understand that there was an organized community life in poor and working-class neighborhoods; poor people have a culture of their own and social strengths that should be enlisted in working with them on social problems. Her presidential address to the National Conference on Charities and Corrections, "Charity and Social Justice," broke new ground for social work by bringing forward a consideration of the economic causes of low industrial standards.[39] Her deep commitment to work with the community, voluntary associations, and social groups and her interest in political action provided a dramatic contrast to Mary Richmond's emphasis on the individual.

Given her strong interest in social reform and her fame, her association with the Progressive party was not surprising. The Hull House group was active in developing the party's platform in 1912, and Addams herself was called upon to second the nomination of Theodore Roosevelt for the presidency. She campaigned for Roosevelt throughout the country on such issues as limitation of working hours, the need for juvenile courts, recognition of labor unions, and factory regulation laws. Many of these ideas came from a report by the Committee on Standards of Living and Labor of the National Conference on Charities and Corrections.[40]

Addams was a pacifist during World War I, and she suffered for it, losing a great deal of her popularity and support. Nonetheless, she continued to support liberal and radical causes even throughout the anticommunist wave of the 1920s, including working for the campaign to free Sacco and Vanzetti, the Italian immigrants and anarchists who were convicted of murder and executed in 1927.

For these activities, she earned the appellations "radical" and "subversive" from Elizabeth Dilling, who authored a famous "exposé" of American radicalism entitled *The Red Network*.[41] Hull

House was considered by reactionaries and superpatriots to be a
"hotbed of radicalism" and "a major link in the subversive network."[42] The American Legion blacklisted Addams as a speaker.
Scabbard and Blade, the publication of the Reserve Officers' Training Corps honorary society, charged that Jane Addams had for
twenty years directed her efforts "to international and subversive
channels until today she stands out as the most dangerous
woman in America."[43] In addition, she was expelled from the
Daughters of the American Revolution (although they had originally made her a life member).

Despite the award of the Nobel prize in 1931, she never re-
gained the popularity and adoration she enjoyed prior to the
war. She even tried, without success, to mobilize support to be
elected President of the National Conference on Social Work in
1923 for its fiftieth anniversary year as a means of restoring her
stature in the field. (Mary Richmond who, because of the
profession's interest in psychiatry, was losing her eminence in social work, also made a try for the presidency of the Conference in
that year and was similarly unsuccessful.)

Only in retrospect do we see the Charity Organization Societies
and settlement houses of Jane Addams and Mary Richmond as
working with clearly articulated opposing ideologies. The former worked with community and the latter with individuals. On
the other hand, both were moralistic, somewhat religious, and
rather Victorian in their outlooks. Today, students would consider them to be conservative. Addams ignored the Great Depression and opposed New Deal reforms, and Richmond was always opposed to government intervention in welfare.

Looking at their earliest work, it is not easy to tell them apart.
Indeed, as Charlotte Towle has noted, Jane Addams and Mary E.
Richmond had a good deal in common:

> They both embodied the spirit of their times. It was a period when
> the central concern of enlightened leaders in social welfare and its
> related fields was to develop the social dimension of the democ-
> racy that the preceding century had sought and won in politics.
> Respect for individuality was pitted against worship of rugged in-

dividualism. Cause was now directed toward bringing about a new order of things as a means of combatting social ills and eliminating evil.[44]

Addams and Richmond first met one another in 1899 when, at Addams's invitation, Richmond attended the Conference of American Settlements held at Hull House. Even at that time the two organizations had become competitors for public support. Addams doubted the efficacy of the COS's formal mission, including its investigatory methods. The COS adherents, including Richmond, questioned the "imprecise conceptualizations of the settlement workers."[45] The significant differences in Richmond's and Addams's views of social work developed over a period of thirty-five years as each of them built upon the strengths of the respective institutions that grew up around them.

Social work seems to have taken shape in a way that neither Addams nor Richmond envisioned entirely. Richmond did not foresee a profession that would have anything like the current commitment social work has to psychotherapy, and Addams underestimated the political barriers to realization of the kind of community support system she tried to foster. Both of them started out with a vision of a profession that would help construct the city on the hill; but instead, at this century's end, we have a profession dedicated to building the church of individual repair.

CHAPTER FOUR

SOCIAL WORK, THE SIREN CALL OF PSYCHIATRY, AND THE GROWTH OF THE WELFARE STATE

———— ◆◈◆ ————

At the end of World War I, social work made a remarkable intellectual leap to embrace psychiatry and then psychoanalysis as its major sources of theory for practice, thus setting the profession's direction for the rest of the century. But in the years before World War I, it would have been difficult to predict with certainty the kind of intellectual base the emerging profession of social work would develop. Social workers utilized a variety of subject matters: eugenics, biology, economics, psychology, and sociology. The best guess anyone could have made for social work's knowledge base would have been sociology. The strongest intellectual contributions to the field came from sociology. Jane Addams was closely associated with sociologists at the University of Chicago, and Mary Richmond was riding high on the prestige she had won as author of the first book on social work practice and as organizer of the Home Service. Had the field capitalized on the latter of these achievements, social work could have become the professional work force for a national system of community-based social care.

Up until 1920, sociology was prominent in social work, and with sociology a professional could, analytically at least, attain a better understanding of poverty and other community problems. With sociology, one could describe the environment: lack of jobs, absence of morals, alcoholism, and poor social standards. Sociology, however, did not provide a theory or a technology that enabled a professional to deal with the individual persons who came to the Charity Organization Societies (COS). And social work was a profession in search of a theory.

The search for a theory began in earnest in 1915, when social workers were stung by a paper presented by Abraham Flexner at the 1915 National Conference of Charities and Corrections, "Is Social Work a Profession?"[1] Dr. Flexner's views about a profession mattered a great deal because he, as author of the influential *Medical Education in the United States and Canada* (1910), had singlehandedly brought about major changes in education for medicine in the United States. His answer to the question about social work's status was "No!" Social work, he said, could not be considered a profession primarily because its practice was not based on a systematic body of knowledge and theory and because it lacked the authority that society gives to professionals to act in particular spheres. The practice of medicine, for example, is based on theory and knowledge from biology, physiology, and chemistry, and physicians have the authority to act on the community's behalf in respect to certifying birth, death, and various illnesses, and for prescribing medicines. Social workers, Flexner pointed out, usually acted as auxiliary staff in assisting other professionals, such as physicians and attorneys, and therefore they did not qualify as professionals in their own right.

Flexner's paper was a great blow to Mary Richmond and her followers. She had tried to adopt the medical model of practice—study, diagnosis, and treatment—and had pushed social work's association with medicine for many years.[2] University-based education for social workers had been developing since 1904 with the establishment by the New York Charity Organization Society of the first one-year graduate program at the New York School of Philanthropy (now Columbia University School of Social Work). Nevertheless, social workers lacked a systematic body of knowledge by which to understand the problems of their clients and to prescribe action by which to help them. (This was more the case with the COS workers than with the settlement house people. Jane Addams had less enthusiasm for professionalism than Mary Richmond. The settlement house workers made use of sociological theories and community analyses, but their ideology made them less receptive to the use of formal training and formal theory. Professionalism, which increased the social distance between the settlers and the residents of the community, would have been counter to their intentions.)

A generation after Flexner's talk, in a famous address to the 1929 National Conference of Social Work, entitled "Social Work: Cause and Function," Porter Lee, director of the New York School of Philanthropy, announced the end of social work as a social movement. The "service," he said (by which he meant the function of professional social work), would henceforth have top priority. The "movement" (by which he meant the cause of social reform and betterment) would have to take a back seat:

> At the moment of its success, the cause tends to transfer its interests and its responsibility to an administrative unit whose responsibility becomes a function of well-organized community life. . . . banner and shibboleth for the cause, the program and manual for the function.[3]

Lee's formulation, giving social work a choice between cause and function, was tricky. He made it sound as if there were only two roads: one of them leading to professionalism and the other to political activism. For Lee, the high road was the route to professionalism, and he had a particular kind of professionalism in mind. He had for many years been among the chief supporters of psychiatric and psychoanalytic kinds of social work. He had written extensively on such phenomena as the "bad effects of repression on the sex instincts" and the importance to the professional of learning about "the effective use of his personality."[4] He wrote of how family dependency "may spring from ignorance, wrong values, shiftlessness, or a broken spirit. Whatever the cause," he said, "successful treatment . . . must include re-education of habit and emphasis upon right standards—through personal influence."[5]

Psychiatry and psychoanalysis were the sources of theory to fill the gap that Flexner had pointed to in his assessment of social work, and they were the sources of the theory needed to implement the function Lee described. But psychiatry and psychoanalysis did not spring full blown on the social work scene.

SOCIAL WORK AND MODERN PSYCHIATRY

Beginning in the middle of the nineteenth century, there were a number of social movements in the United States for the improvement of care of the mentally ill, as well as movements for general self-improvement and self-realization and for curing physical illnesses. It is a curiosity that social work had relatively little to do with these popular movements for mind cure and other talking cures until the middle of the twentieth century. One would have thought that there would have been a closer kinship between social workers and groups like the phrenologists, Christian Scientists, spiritualists, mesmerists, and the positive thinkers. Both kinds of work were concerned with human betterment, and both opened up new career lines for women. But there was little affinity between the two groups. Social workers, the Charity Organizationists, and the settlement house leaders had no institutional interest in the mind cures or the work of the positive thinkers. One reason is that the early formal leadership of the social welfare and social work movements was predominantly males, many of them clergymen and physicians who viewed ideologies of the mind curists and positive thinkers as anathema. The mind curists and positive thinkers believed that people, especially women, should exercise greater control over their own lives; they offered alternatives to established medical practice; and they were considered to be anticlerical because they elevated self-development and self-reliance above divine guidance. Occasional references to the mind cure movements in the early social work literature are pejorative, made almost as epithets.

Although social work presented the potential for new careers and for economic and social liberation for women, this possibility remained subterranean for a long time. It took thirty-seven years for the National Conference on Charities and Corrections to select a woman for its president, and she was not an ordinary woman. By that time Jane Addams had become an international powerhouse.

Another reason for the separation between the two groups is that both the social workers and the settlement workers of the nineteenth century were primarily interested in creating healthy environments. The mind curists and positive thinkers were entirely focused on creating healthy individuals. Some of their ideas would have been considered entirely too self-indulgent by nineteenth-century social workers.

But the social workers of the 1920s took to psychiatry like ducks to water. The transition from Victorian Poor Law morality regarding indolence and sloth to Freudian thinking about instinctual and unconscious motivation is not difficult to trace. Supporting social work's strong desire to associate itself with a medical type of intervention were several other late-nineteenth-century social movements for mental hygiene, sexual hygiene, and child guidance that had been gathering force in the United States. The mental hygiene movement, for example, was spurred by Clifford Beers, an ex–mental patient whose autobiographical book, *A Mind That Found Itself*, published in 1908, was a best seller.[6] Beers, who is credited with founding the mental hygiene movement, was a major speaker at the National Conference on Charities and Corrections in 1909.

On the practical side, World War I had left a large number of veterans who were suffering from what was then called shell shock and today would be called posttraumatic stress syndrome. Care and treatment of these veterans opened up many job possibilities for social workers. Together, the impact of the new mental health movements and the care of the veterans provided a line of thought for social workers that neatly filled the knowledge and theory gap gnawing at the social workers who were concerned about professionalization. It was a line of thought that would direct the profession for the rest of the century.

American psychiatry in 1919 was not yet dominated by psychoanalytic thinking. The psychiatry that social workers took to at that time was based on theories of modern psychiatry that had been developing for fifty years in Europe. Social workers learned about and practiced this psychiatry under the tutelage of such physicians as Adolf Meyer, A. A. Brill, Richard Cabot, Lawson Lowry, and Marion Kenworthy.

Until the mid-nineteenth century, mental illness was perceived to be primarily the result of sin and demons, or brain lesions and neurological malfunctions.[7] "Lunatics" of all types and ages, with both functional and organic disorders (e.g., psychotics, epileptics, the feebleminded and senile, and cases of general paresis), were for the most part cared for indiscriminately in almshouses, lunatic asylums, and jails.

By the latter part of the nineteenth century, the mentally ill in the United States were being cared for primarily in state hospitals. The development of this institutional system represented a great advance in its day. Psychiatry, a relatively young profession, evolved primarily from the nineteenth-century physicians who administered the state hospitals.[8] The great reforms in caring for the mentally ill (e.g., moral treatment, no restraint, and the open door) were introduced by these psychiatrists, who constituted a significant part of what Albert Deutsch referred to as the "culture of curability."[9]

A number of new ideas about the relation of mental illness to unconscious mental processes and sexual drives, which had been developing in Europe from the work of Friedrich Mesmer, Francis Galton, Jean Martin Charcot, Pierre Janet, and Sigmund Freud, were absorbed only gradually by American psychiatry. The bulk of clinical psychiatrists were either apathetic about or hostile to the theories of Freud and his followers until after World War II. The somatic therapies (e.g., insulin and shock therapy and prefrontal lobotomy) were introduced more readily in the state hospitals.

The shift in thinking of American social workers stemming from their interest in psychiatry (and, later, psychoanalysis) is important enough for us to provide a sampling of social workers' thoughts over those years as they made the transition to psychiatric casework. For example, at the turn of the century W. H. Mc-Clain had done research on and written about the relation between "defective character and dependence." At approximately the same time, A. W. Gutridge, a charity organizationist, was saying, "Whether or not material relief is needed is incidental; whether or not their lives conform to our standards of morality is incidental; *the cure has to do with personality.*"[10]

By 1917, Mary Richmond was on the defensive for calling her book "*social*" rather than "*individual*" diagnosis.[11] To add insult to injury, in 1918 E. E. Southard, a physician, presented a paper, "The Kingdom of Evils," in which he reanalyzed the cases Richmond discussed in *Social Diagnosis*. He reported that he found "more than half the Richmond group to be afflicted in an important sense with some one or other of the *Morbi* [diseases]. The great size of the psychopathic fraction in Miss Richmond's book is of particular value to us."[12] Southard concluded that it was necessary to "replace the family as the unit of social inquiry with the individual as the unit." Southard did acknowledge, though, that his view of social case analysis was "medicated."

In 1920, immediately after the war, C. M. Campbell asserted in an address to social workers engaged with juvenile delinquents:

> It was not possible to understand the war neuroses of the soldiers, nor is it possible to understand the neuroses of everyday life, without studying the conflicting instincts, the emotional problems, the painful memories of the patient, and the same principles at the basis of the study of the neuroses have to be applied to the study of the delinquent episode or career.[13]

Mary Jarrett, director of social service at the Boston Psychiatric Hospital and one of the founders of the Smith College training program in psychiatric social work, presented a paper at the 1919 conference. In "The Psychiatric Thread Running Through All Social Case Work," she held that since the adaptation of the individual to his or her environment (the accepted goal of social casework at the time) depended on the mental makeup of that person, the study of the "mental life" was fundamental to social casework. Although Jarrett allowed that physical and economic factors affecting the individual were also fundamental to social casework, the emphasis on the individual's psychological construction was clearly a new direction for social work.[14]

Social workers of the 1920s were ecstatic at having found something as significant as psychiatry to practice with. Jessie Taft, writing in 1922, was exhilarated over the discovery of psychiatry:

> What gives the case worker the right to take on so unlimited a responsibility [to use psychiatric knowledge in dealing with children in placement]? . . . What right has case work to go on experimenting *with life itself?* . . . There is as yet no justification in conscious knowledge or technique; but the work is there to be done. There is no other profession to do it. . . . The position of the case

worker is at once the most thrilling and the most terrifying in the whole gamut of scientific or semi-scientific undertakings which seek to gain social control in terms of the behavior of the human organism.[15]

Many social workers began to incorporate the psychology of John Dewey and the behaviorism of H. A. Overstreet into their work, and some of them became increasingly interested in the psychoanalytic theories of Sigmund Freud, Otto Rank, and their interpreters in this country.[16] In the 1920s this new focus traveled with psychiatric social workers as they helped to inspire the child guidance movement and took jobs outside the confines of hospitals in family casework agencies.[17] According to Virginia Robinson, then director of the Pennsylvania School of Social and Health Work, this decade saw "the emergence of relationship" in the profession, that is, the relationship—conscious and unconscious—between caseworker and client.[18]

Although the psychiatric social workers were yet to have a journal of their own with which to spread the new wisdom, publications of interest to social workers at the time, such as the *Family* and *Mental Hygiene*, included discussions of the changing horizons of social casework, some written by psychiatrists and psychiatric social workers, as well as numerous book reviews of relevant psychiatric and psychoanalytic literature. In her 1926 article, "The Relation of Psychiatry to Social Work," Jessie Taft, director of the Child Study Department at the Children's Aid Society of Pennsylvania, provides a historical account of the beginnings of psychiatric social work and the interest in mental hygiene, asserting that this represents the "birth of an epoch-making movement."[19] After discussing the impact of the interest in psychological interpretation upon other trends in social work (e.g., child guidance and family casework), Taft concluded:

One of the main objectives ahead is to provide in our schools of social work a training in casework theory and practice which is organically related to the psychiatric interpretation of behavior in every detail of social diagnosis and treatment. What shall be the content of this psychiatric viewpoint, only the future will determine; but that it will broaden and deepen and take into account more and more the field of unconscious motivation there is no doubt.

It is not for nothing that the word psycho-analytic appears boldly this year for the first time on a National Conference program.[20]

The psychiatric/psychoanalytic trend exerted a considerable influence on some in the profession and began to play an important role in theoretical discussions of practice in areas outside psychiatric social work; however, it was not yet a predominant trend in casework practice in the 1920s. Psychiatric social workers were a small but influential minority in the profession, and there was occasional talk of private practice, but it was not a priority issue at any national conference of the profession during that decade, nor would it be until the 1950s.[21] On the other hand, judging from a review of their literature, it appears that early on, psychiatric social workers embraced psychoanalysis and the developing personality psychologies at some relative expense to both medical and social diagnostic approaches. They also took a much greater interest in the private practice of their craft than did their counterparts in other social work specializations.

Most of the seminal figures in psychiatric social work during the 1920s were heavily influenced by the psychoanalytic view and communicated this to the field through the written word as well as through their teaching at various schools of social work.[22] When the AAPSW (American Association of Psychiatric Social Workers) first published the *News-Letter* in July 1931, the lead article, "Changing Goals of Psychiatric Social Work," contained references to the primary importance that the broader psychological aspects of the client-worker relationship had assumed and the increasingly important role of psychoanalytic concepts in the social worker's thinking.[23] A year later, the president of the association, Elizabeth Brockett, in discussing the focal points of current thinking about psychiatric social work, noted that there was "less dependence upon procedures borrowed from medicine, including a breaking away from a routine approach in history taking" and an increased "tendency to study technique in light of knowledge coming from psychiatry and mainly the psychoanalytic school."[24] A perusal of the *News-Letter* during the 1930s finds numerous book reviews of psychoanalytic literature as well as articles by Otto Rank, Karen Horney, and Franz Alexander.

It does not appear that psychiatric social workers simply followed the lead of American psychiatry in incorporating the psychoanalytic view. On the contrary, literature of the period indicates that in the 1920s, Freud and his followers were less widely accepted by physicians than by the social workers with whom they worked.[25]

Psychiatric social work education from its inception relied heavily on the teaching of professionals who were sympathetic to psychoanalysis. Bertha Reynolds, a prominent figure in social work during the 1920s and 1930s and a graduate of the first summer course in psychiatric social work held at Smith College in 1918, had this to say about the attitude of her classmates:

> Our concentration on therapy, rather than on the social accompaniments of the patient's illness, was brought out when the class was eagerly awaiting the assignments for six months of field practice. When the announcement was finally made in August, those who could not be accommodated in army hospitals or Red Cross units, but were sent to the New York Charity Organization Society, were bitterly disappointed. "We did not come here to learn social work but psychotherapy," they said.[26]

Noting that social work students had had more hours of lectures in psychiatry than were given in most medical schools, Mary Jarrett warned them to "never speak of Freud" in front of doctors, at least not until they were sure of a sympathetic audience, and then only with "becoming modesty."[27] That the social workers thus trained would persist in their interest in the dynamics of the unconscious and focus on the creation of a therapeutic relationship with the client in spite of conflicting tendencies found within mainstream psychiatry attests to the feelings of discovery and mastery they derived from these new ideas.

There was no shortage of clients for those with these bold new ideas. In 1924, Edward D. Lynde spoke to the National Conference of Social Work of an innovative approach to social casework. A family agency in Cincinnati, he reported, had engaged a psychiatric caseworker, and in just one year the number of "diagnosed or suspected mental cases" jumped from 4 percent to 15 percent. Over a four-year period the number of such cases increased more than tenfold.[28]

Social workers continued to worship at the altar of psycho-

analysis into the deepest and darkest moments of the Great Depression and World War II. Grace Marcus, one of the great teachers of social casework in that era, exulted throughout the decades
about the centrality of psychoanalytic thought in solving social
problems. For example, in 1935 she wrote pridefully of what she
termed the "psychiatric deluge," as a result of which

> the casework method of study and treatment underwent inner
> corrections inspired by psychoanalytic experience with methods
> of studying the mind. . . . Aesthetic, moral, and conventional so-
> cial standards became irrelevant criteria. . . . The place of psycho-
> analytic insight in case work is analogous to the place of physiol-
> ogy in medical science, basic to any responsible understanding of
> the function of the individual as a psychobiological organism, in-
> trinsic in all diagnosis and treatment, but not necessarily explicit
> in the spoken word or written record.[29]

Psychiatric social work's having developed first as an adjunct
to psychiatry in the care of the mentally ill in state hospitals
where a majority of patients suffered from somatic conditions
created a clear condition for proscribing the independent involvement of social workers and clinical psychologists in psychotherapy.[30] In order to practice psychotherapy, psychologists and
social workers had to be subservient to physicians, a condition
that continued until the mid-twentieth century.

In the 1930s, psychoanalytic treatment was adopted by some
physicians practicing privately. Unlike treatment in mental hospitals, which involved primarily physiological, neurological, and
pharmacological technologies, psychoanalytic therapy was a
"talking cure" that could be employed by nonphysicians and,
hence, was attractive to nonmedical health professionals, such as
social workers and psychologists. As it turned out, in the United
States, psychoanalysis came to exercise influence on concepts of
mental health and explanations of behavior disorders far beyond
that of any other theoretical framework. The adoption of the
Freudian paradigm was ultimately instrumental in strengthening the capacities of social workers and clinical psychologists to
engage in psychotherapy.[31]

Psychiatry and psychoanalysis remained central to social work
and social work education through the 1940s. The depression

and the world war drew the profession back momentarily to social concerns and provided a social context for the emergence of
social group work and community organization as social work
specializations. During the early depression years, a large proportion of social work rank and file became radical and militant.
To take just one of many examples, in 1934, in a virtual call to
arms, Mary van Kleeck asked social workers for

> alignment with other workers, not drawing their inspiration from
> the relationship of social worker to client, but rather identifying
> themselves as fellow-workers looking toward more action, clearer
> facing of the issues, and demands which are not tempered to the
> "temper" of the administration and Congress, but to the needs of
> the working people, whose standards of living should be the pri-
> mary and indeed the sole concern of all branches of social work.[32]

For another example of how quickly social workers were radical-
ized by the great depression, the Family Society of Philadelphia
in1930 reclassified all of its current cases and found that more
than half the families in treatment were suffering from economic
deprivations rather than the psychological problems perceived
by the social caseworkers.[33] This turnabout of the reclassification
of Mary Richmond's cases in "The Kingdom of Evils" was fair
play, a bit of poetic justice, and a good illustration of how the
emerging profession of social work is responsive to economic
and political changes in the environment.

SOCIAL WORK AND THE POPULAR PSYCHOTHERAPIES

Although the popular psychotherapies had been bubbling along
in American life for over 150 years, social work did not incorporate them until after 1950. On the way, social work connected
with modern psychiatry in the 1920s, psychoanalysis in the
1930s, and humanistic psychology in the 1950s. The history of social work can be viewed as a one-hundred-year preparation for
incorporation into the psychotherapy industry (figure 2).

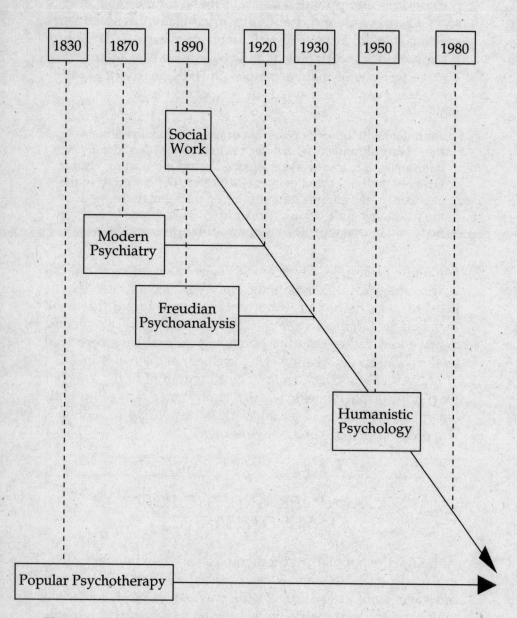

Figure 2 *Social Work and the Psychotherapies*

Carl Rogers opened the way for nonmedically based psycho-therapy.[34] His client-oriented psychotherapy represents a clear break with psychoanalysis; the latter had been preempted by physicians, whereas the former had emerged in, and was squarely in the purview of, psychologists. It was easily adapted to the practice of psychiatric social work independent of physicians.

Rogers helped lay the foundation for what is today called humanistic psychology. There is very little that is theoretical or empirically based in the humanistically oriented psychologies of Carl Rogers, Abraham Maslow, Fritz Perls, Otto Pollack, and a host of others. ("Theory" is used here in the sense of testable and tested propositions that enable one to predict.) However, there is, in humanistically oriented psychology, a powerful attitude and belief system about how to build and reconstruct the self: "you can do it; you're wonderful and good; there is richness in you; if it feels good on you, it's okay." These are the fundamental beliefs of those secular priests we mentioned earlier, and these ideas are the extension as well of the early-1800s beliefs of the mind curists in the perfectibility of the individual and the later-1800s optimistic beliefs of the positive thinkers. From client-oriented psychotherapy based on humanistic psychology, it is only a hop, skip, and a jump to the popular psychotherapies. You find them all advertised together, with a good many of them offered by licensed clinical social workers, in monthly free issues of *Open Exchange* and *Common Ground*, your local newspaper, and the newsletters of the state chapters of the National Association of Social Workers.

THE EMERGENCE OF SOCIAL WELFARE AS AN INSTITUTION

The period following the end of the depression and World War II up to the 1960s was one of consolidation and development of the technology of social work practice. The relatively young specialization of social group work was gradually absorbed into the clinical side of social work. There was significant growth of doc-

toral programs in social work, and this resulted in a vast increase
in the amount of research done on social work and social welfare,
the bulk of it dealing with the subjects of social policy and behavioral treatments. Most clinical social workers who seek Ph.D.s in
order to hang out a shingle and call themselves "Doctor" obtain
them at institutes and universities where one can attend part time
and where the research requirements are not heavy.

There is a big split in the field between social workers who are
interested in social welfare, social policy, and public programs,
and those who are interested in clinical practice. The former tend
to be oriented to and interested in practical social supports and
public service. The clinicians tend to be more interested in individual diagnosis, intrapersonal development, treatment processes, and the uses of the therapeutic relationship. These two
sets of social workers in social work education tolerate one another. The social policy people need the profession, and the clinicians need the policy and programs adherents in order to be able
to continue to call themselves social workers. With only one exception, education for both social work and social welfare in the
United States takes place at the same educational institutions. (The
one exception in the United States is the Florence Heller School
for Advanced Studies in Social Welfare at Brandeis University,
which is devoted exclusively to the study of social policies and
programs and is not involved at all with social work practice.)

Social welfare today is an enormous enterprise. Even with the
conservative Reagan and Bush administrations, there has been
no significant change in the basic structures of income-support
programs. The neoconservative 1980s, in fact, reaffirmed the legitimate role of national governments in ensuring citizens a degree of economic security when they become ill, disabled, unemployed, and otherwise dependent. Recipients in the major
programs—social security and Medicare—continued to do as
well, and in some cases better, during that period. There was,
nevertheless, a significant chipping away at the levels of benefits
provided to some groups. Benefits for Aid to Families with Dependent Children (AFDC) and general assistance (GA) recipients
eroded by about 42 percent during the Reagan and Bush administrations.[35]

Additionally, the years of neoconservatism have been discouraging to social workers. Social work has suffered from being poorly financed and unloved, and public support has been at a low ebb. But even so, the public remained willing to provide resources to prevent economic dependency. There continues to be public discontent about the welfare system as a whole, which is, according to some outstanding social welfare scholars, frequently irrational, wasteful, and unfair. Many of our most liberal analysts have pointed to the need for reform of the system of social welfare, an objective that has eluded both liberal and neoconservative administrations over recent decades.[36]

The basic structure of income-support programs is fairly secure, and the idea of national responsibility for income security is fairly well institutionalized.[37] There will be continued scholarly work on and debate about these programs and perennial questions about the level of benefits provided, the costs to the economy of these programs, the conditions of eligibility, and so forth. Income supports have come to be perceived as a significant part of the economy; indeed, most benefits are now indexed to the cost of living, a clear indication of the extent to which these supports have come to be perceived as necessary and normative.

Social work as a profession is enormous. Public expenditures on the social services (exclusive of the income-maintenance programs) are sizable. Until the 1960s, most of the states administered public assistance primarily as a money-benefits program. There were variations among the states in the kinds of personnel used and the kinds of social services offered to recipients. Most states conditioned the receipt of benefits on acceptance by recipients of social casework services. In some places these services consisted of regulatory surveillance, primarily of AFDC recipients, including investigation of applicants' eligibility and home visiting (and sometimes midnight raids) to ensure that a "welfare mother" did not have a "man in the house" and that recipients continued to be eligible and were living "properly." In other places social workers fulfilled more enabling, supportive, and therapeutic functions.

The 1962 amendments to the Social Security Act provided federal funds for state provision of intensive social casework services by professionals to AFDC recipients. The objective of these services was to "rehabilitate" recipients and thereby reduce their economic dependency. This objective was not attained. Rather, between 1963 and 1971, the welfare roles expanded and federal grants to states for social services increased from $19 million to $740 million.[38]

The failure of the social services program to reduce economic dependency cooled considerably Congress's interest in social casework. The next legislative efforts to deal with economic dependency, the Economic Opportunity Act of 1964 and the 1967 amendments to the Social Security Act, enabled the states to provide a more comprehensive array of social services, including casework, day care centers, and work training.[39]

The increase in social service expenditures between 1963 and 1971 was due in part to the greater number of welfare recipients. It was due also to legislative loopholes through which the states transferred to the federal government the costs of many services that had been financed locally. When Congress received an estimate of $4.7 billion for the costs of social services programs in 1973, it enacted Title XX of the Social Security Act, placing a ceiling of $2.4 billion on federal expenditures for social services.

Title XX established a framework for the states to provide comprehensive social services on a universal basis (to everyone in need of them, regardless of their income). States could provide services to public assistance (AFDC and Supplementary Security Income) recipients as well as to people who were eligible on the basis of insufficient income. Some services, such as family planning and protective services, were available to everyone without regard to income.

In 1974, when Title XX went into effect and the states reported on their programs, it was found that 1,212 services had been offered in the following categories:

Adoption services

Case management services

Congregate meals

Counseling services

Adult day care services

Child day care services

Employment, education, and training services

Family planning services

Foster care services for adults

Foster care services for children

Health-related and home health services

Home-based services

Home-delivered meals

Housing services

Information and referral services

Legal services

Pregnancy and parenting services for young parents

Prevention and intervention services

Protective services for adults

Protective services for children

Recreational services

Residential treatment services

Special services for the developmentally disabled, the blind, and the physically disabled

Special services for juvenile delinquents

Transportation services

Other services[40]

Although Title XX provided a framework for a comprehensive system of personal social services, the objectives were never fully implemented. Congress maintained a budget ceiling on the program from 1974 to 1981. Then, under the Reagan administration's 1981 Omnibus Budget Reconciliation Act, Title XX was replaced by the Social Services Block Grant (SSBG), which eliminated all requirements that the federal government had placed upon the states for receipt of Title XX funds, and federal support for the program was reduced considerably. Support for other social service programs such as Medicaid and the school lunch program was also reduced.

Currently, because of inadequate federal reporting requirements, it is difficult to assess what social services the states are
providing. It appears that since 1981 there has been a marked increase in the offering of personal social services on a voluntary
and a for-profit basis.

Thus, although the social services that are offered publicly in
the United States constitute an enormous enterprise, the system
lacks the public and political support enjoyed by the system of
income maintenance. Unfortunately, too, this major institution
has been largely ignored by the profession of social work. In most
state and county agencies, caseloads are too large, and the is difficult and sometimes dangerous. These are some of the reasons
that many professional social workers do not seek careers in the
publicly supported services. The cause-and-effect relations are
circular: the dearth of professionals in these services leads to a
decline in professionalism, which adds to the difficulty of recruiting new professionals. In the United States, the organized profession of social work has never perceived of itself as having any
special responsibility for the publicly supported social services,
and those public social services have languished accordingly.
With so many of its members preoccupied with an interest in private practice and psychotherapy, the profession does not find the
publicly supported social services to be especially fertile soil in
which to take root.

Education for the profession of social work is an enormous enterprise. There are three degree levels at which one can be educated for social work, with approximately one hundred graduate
schools of social work in the United States and over four hundred
bachelor's level programs. Not surprisingly, students at the
bachelor's level are perceived by most social work educators to
be preparing for work in the publicly supported social services;
graduate students are perceived to be preparing for specialized
work, typically a euphemism for psychotherapy.

Social workers have a national professional association, the
National Association of Social Workers (NASW), which was established in 1955. In 1992, NASW, with 140,000 members, is one
of the largest professional associations in the world. It manages
to create a semblance of national unity only with great difficulty.
The members of the National Societies of Clinical Social Work

and several associations based on race, ethnicity, and religion are constantly competing for control of the profession's direction.

In 1957, when psychiatric social work came into full bloom, Marion Sanders wrote a stinging critique of social work, saying that it was "a profession chasing its tail."[41] In the 1990s social work has grown a rather large private psychotherapeutic tail and now stands in danger of being wagged by it.

CHAPTER FIVE

THE MOVEMENT OF SOCIAL WORK INTO PRIVATE PRACTICE

(AND AWAY FROM THE POOR)

————

Forty years ago, two leaders in the fields of social work and psychiatry had this to say:

> At present, psychiatrists, social workers and psychologists are all quarreling among themselves like jealous children, over who has the right to "do therapy," and who does the best job. The unfortunate patient seems in danger of being pulled to pieces by us professional wolves in sheep's clothing. Quite often, however, he gets well in spite of us, which should give us pause to consider whether we are not all taking ourselves a bit too seriously. We would do well to admit that no one profession has the answer now. Then perhaps, we could get beyond our sibling rivalry to the point of using the pooled intelligence and experience of all three professions to find a really practical answer, that will enable any psychiatrist, social worker or psychologist who is interested in therapy and fitted for it, to become qualified through a recognized training.[1]

> If it were possible or desirable to extend training in psychotherapy to non-medical personnel, the caseworker is indeed in a strategically placed position. However, I think there is a greater need at this time for well-qualified caseworkers practicing their own profession than for any ambitious expansion in the number of therapists. We have still to learn how much the caseworker can contribute through his own methods to a lessening of human misery. There have never been enough well-trained caseworkers to begin to touch the problem; it would seem a pity to divert any large numbers of them into psychotherapy.[2]

106

We agree wholeheartedly. The professional wolves in sheep's clothing (which now include the "marriage, family, and child counselors") are still fighting territorial battles with each other over the psychotherapeutic pie, and there are still too few well-trained social workers in public and voluntary agencies to deal practically with glaring social problems.

On the other hand, some things have changed, although not for the better. Social work has become the largest single mental health profession, and the development of the private practice of social work has become one of the most significant trends in the profession.[3] Confluent with these developments there has been an increasing tendency of the profession to use its political power to support licensing of clinical social workers and third-party payments for social workers who are so licensed, to the relative neglect of efforts to improve the lot of social workers employed in the public social services and their clients.

How is it that so many social workers have come to see their primary role as the provision of psychotherapeutic services, and why has this increasingly taken on the form of private practice? We believe that the answer can be found through an understanding of some of the characteristics of professions in general and an appreciation of the subtle effects that the American ideology of individualism has had in shaping the employment options of social workers. We will show how the development of the private practice of social work parallels and reflects the growth in importance of the therapeutic approach within the profession and we will examine some of the unfortunate results.

PRIVATE PRACTICE AND PROFESSIONALIZATION

One evening in 1896, Mary Richmond was catching up on some work after the Baltimore Charity Organization Society (COS) for which she worked had closed for the day. Responding to a knock on the door, she found one of the agency's volunteers, who had a personal problem she wanted to discuss with Richmond. Richmond readily obliged. The generous provision of good advice was something for which she was well known. After the talk, the woman gratefully offered Richmond three dollars. Although taken aback by the offer, Richmond accepted the money. She was employed by the COS, but this money was offered to her for her own time by someone who was not a client of the agency. She decided that she could use the money to help the agency's true clients.[4] Years later, when writing about the potential for the private practice of social casework, Richmond remarked that "the skill here described can be utilized quite as well in the homes of the rich as in those of the poor, that in the one as in the other, personality can be thwarted and retarded, developed and enriched."[5]

The development of social work private practice can be considered one reflection of the professionalization of social work. Some sociological treatments of this subject describe a profession as an occupation that exhibits certain characteristics: a defined and substantial knowledge base; a prolonged training period; a code of ethics regulating relationships between professionals and their clients; a "professional culture" reinforced by a professional association; a commitment on the part of its members to the calling of the profession; and the professional's right to exercise professional autonomy in relation to clients.[6] Some who hold this view have argued that not all occupations meet all of the criteria of a profession to the same degree.[7] Following from this is the idea that there is a continuum of occupations ranging from the ideal professions at one end (e.g., law and medicine) to unskilled occupations at the other. In discussions of this sort, social work is often placed somewhere in the middle of the continuum and considered a semiprofession.[8]

Other theorists have advanced a political-economic analysis of the division of labor, arguing that the characteristics that appear to be typical of professions are really part of an occupational strategy, carried out by groups of people who hold professional or managerial jobs, that is intended to stabilize the role of these occupations and gain them a privileged economic status.[9] From this perspective "a profession is not an occupation, but a means of controlling an occupation."[10] Presumably, the control that the profession seeks to exert is equivalent to establishing a monopoly over the production, distribution, and consumption of a service.

In the case of psychotherapy, the turf battles over licensing and insurance reimbursement between the various groups of mental health practitioners can be seen as examples of profession building.

The legal and medical professions have established relative hegemony over the areas of service they provide, both of which have traditionally been paid for primarily with private funds provided by the recipients of the service (or, more recently, private insurance). Provision of services to clients who cannot pay for services themselves (e.g., legal aid clients or Medicaid recipients) has always been a relatively low priority within these professions, as evidenced by the dearth of such services.

Unlike the "ideal professions," social work's traditional clientele was not primarily middle-class individuals who could pay for a service provided by an independent practitioner. For example, the hypothetical mother described in chapter 2 who wants to get her children back might very well find herself benefiting from the services of a social worker, but it is unlikely that she will be paying for those services. Indeed, it has been primarily the middle classes that have supported social services for those who could not pay. This support has come either voluntarily through charitable contributions and volunteerism or through taxes to support the public social services. Thus, for the most part, the social worker based in a public or nonprofit voluntary agency has been able to provide a service to poor people only with the tacit approval of those elements of society least likely to need that service: the middle and upper classes. Herein lies the rub for social workers: in developing a profession for themselves, which services are worth attempting to control, and how do they control them? It is one thing to retain professional autonomy in relationships with clients who are paying directly for a service that they want (e.g., relationships between lawyers and their clients or therapists and their patients). It is quite another to attempt to maintain the same autonomy when providing a service to clients who cannot always expect to get what they want, given that the social worker must keep in mind the demands of the society that sanctions and pays for the provision of that service. For example, the social worker assigned with helping our hypothetical mother to regain custody of her children must also keep in mind society's sometimes conflicting demand that the child be protected from harm. One attempt at a solution to this dilemma has been the development of the private practice of psychotherapy by social workers.

Mary Richmond's acceptance of three dollars for her individual help with what were described as personal problems has been characterized as the first example of the private practice of social work.[11] While it was an extremely brief foray into private practice, it provides a prophetic example of the trends that the private practice of social work would exhibit in the future. It was neither public relief nor a typical social service that Richmond provided but a form of talking cure. Furthermore, Richmond's client was a middle-class volunteer who, unlike the clients of the organization for which she worked, was able to pay for the service provided.

An exploration of the first attempts by psychiatric social workers to develop a private practice of social work between World Wars I and II provides an opportunity to clarify some of the unique roots of the private practice of social work and a baseline against which to evaluate later events. We have already described how the 1920s and 1930s represented a time of growing interest in psychiatric and psychoanalytic theory within the social work profession. We will also find that the private practice of social work developed as the practice of psychotherapy by social workers and that the movement into private practice by social workers represented a shift from the provision of services to the poor, the delinquent, the dispossessed, and the disabled to the provision of psychotherapy to primarily middle-class clients who could afford to pay for it.

PSYCHIATRIC SOCIAL WORK AND THE EARLY YEARS OF PRIVATE PRACTICE

In 1926, the American Association of Social Workers (AASW) took up a request by its Philadelphia chapter to discuss the issue of private practice. The AASW executive committee decided to elicit membership response to the idea of private social work practice by sending a memorandum to all chapters posing several questions and elucidating some essential conditions for this type of social work generally.[12] There appears to have been no further discussion of the memo, and the subject was not taken up by the national professional association again until the 1950s.

At the same time, psychiatric social workers were taking a greater interest in the possibilities presented by private practice. In 1927, the year after its formation, the American Association of Psychiatric Social Workers (AAPSW) formed the Committee on Private Psychiatric Social Work.[13] It was not coincidental that psychiatric social workers were the first of the emerging social work specialties to take an active interest in private practice. This was consistent with the growth of a trend especially prominent in psychiatric social work: the shift from an emphasis on the manipulation of the individual's environment to manipulation of the individual's personality and the relationship between social worker and client.

An equally profound change was taking place in respect to the clientele of family caseworkers. More and more of the clients of family caseworkers were members of the middle class. Although the Great Depression would shortly turn back the clock on this development, it is interesting to see what issues arose as this potential market for social work services became apparent. As early as 1926, some professionals in the family welfare field recognized that many of their clients were not recipients of material relief and attributed this change in the population requesting services to limitations on immigration and increasing economic stability.[14] Many social workers began to believe that the therapeutically oriented skills that they had acquired were potentially applicable to all families regardless of social class and that it was the responsibility, if not the destiny, of social workers to use these skills wherever possible. As early as 1926, Francis Taussig, executive director of the United Hebrew Charities of New York, raised the possibility of pay clinics and private practitioners "in the art of helping families."[15]

Dorothy Kahn's frank analysis in 1928 of the budding interest in private practice in "The Future of Family Social Work" clearly identifies the source of that interest in the interaction between the desire for more control of the worker-client relationship on the one hand, and the recognition of the potential middle-class market for social work services on the other. In discussing hypothetical wishes for the future of family social work, she writes of the desire to know "infinitely more about the human stuff of our job" and "to be free to enter into a more direct relationship with our client."[16] Making note of the relatively poor compensation and professional status of social workers, she alludes to the potential—and potential contradiction—presented by the new clientele:

> We are found pleading pathetically for attention to the growing population of "service only" cases. We point out with ill-disguised satisfaction that a certain well-known person or member of the board has asked us to treat his family problem—privately, of course.[17]

Kahn recognized the appeal of private practice for social caseworkers similar to that enjoyed by the medical profession. Her prophecy as to the direction the profession would take over the next fifty years was a description of that private practice:

> Social case work, better named, will replace the fortuitous specialties of our day. The practitioner will supersede the agency, which has both nurtured and protected him. His relation to his client will have the sanction of reality. He will be no agent, no dispenser of gifts, but a teacher of eager, thoughtful students of life. . . . The maladjusted worker and the unhappy family will come to the practitioner when service is required, but there will be no necessary correlation between their material and their spiritual need.[18]

Even at this early date, one is tempted to guess that, given Kahn's description, social casework's "better name" would be "psychotherapy."

Much early social work practice in psychiatric settings consisted of the provision of family histories and social studies, which were acquired through structured interviews for use by the psychiatrist. The psychoanalytic approach allowed for much more creativity and thoughtfulness on the part of the worker conducting such interviews. In a segment of the social work profession that was made up almost entirely of women working mostly for male psychiatrists, it is not surprising that an approach that placed central importance on the deepening of the independent relationship between the caregiver and the client would find great appeal. The relative autonomy of the psychiatric social worker, which was at least suggested by the psychoanalytic view, also may have contributed to the movement of some psychiatric social workers into other social work fields.[19]

Thus, much of the appeal of psychoanalysis likely resulted from the fact that the therapeutic relationship opened a way of viewing social work that provided for more individual autonomy on the part of the worker.

Expressing this desire for autonomy and a fascination with the power of the therapeutic relationship, psychiatric social workers took a greater interest in private practice than did any of the other social work specialties of the day. The AAPSW's Committee on Private Psychiatric Social Work carried out its work from 1927 until at least 1932, when the last mention of it is made in the *News-Letter*. According to a survey conducted by the committee, children and adolescents constituted the largest group treated in private practice. The survey also indicated that a sliding scale of fees was in use, hourly service generally receiving from three to five dollars and full-time weekly service from fifty to one hundred dollars with all expenses. At these rates, private practice would have appeared to be a high-paying opportunity, with salaries ranging from about the average for a psychiatric social worker of that period to over twice that average.[20] Furthermore, this practice was unusual in that social service agencies did not commonly charge their clients fees until the mid-1940s.[21]

Although much of what was described as private practice in those days was private only in the sense that the social worker was employed by a psychiatrist who was in private practice rather than in the employ of an agency, there is no doubt that much of this work allowed for far more autonomy on the part of the worker, including the relatively independent conduct of psychotherapeutic treatment.[22] It seems likely that some psychiatric social workers were seeing clients on even more independent terms than those described. After being requested by the AAPSW to comment on the relationship between psychiatry and psychiatric social work, Bertha Reynolds delivered an address to the annual meeting in 1934 consisting of an allegorical tale about a middle-aged man, Dr. Psychiatry, and a young woman, P.S.W. (psychiatric social worker). In the story, Dr. Psychiatry has clearly been rejected by his kin (the medical profession) who consider him "queer," and P.S.W. is "loath to admit her connection" to her family (the social work profession) who are too closely associated with poverty. While Reynolds comments on the fact that since 1930 (the onset of the Great Depression) Dr. Psychiatry and P.S.W. "do not set up a menage together as often as they once did," she also describes the opening of a "mysterious office" in the neighborhood where people go "one at a time, each on the same day and hour each week," to "just talk." Reynolds expresses that she is afraid Dr. Psychiatry does not know about this office and that P.S.W. "takes some of his things over there and sells them."[23] This may be what later supporters and chroniclers of the private practice movement mean when they assert that early private practitioners went underground after the AAPSW refused to pursue the idea of private social work practice.[24] Levenstein did discover several examples in the NASW's historical files dating from this period referring to social workers in private practice, most of whom are either identified as psychiatric social workers or whose descriptions imply as much.[25]

Lee Rabinowitz Steiner, a psychiatric social worker in New York City, is the only social worker we know of who started her own private practice prior to World War II and decided to discuss frankly her experiences in the literature.[26] Steiner's reasons for undertaking this experiment and the course that it took provide substantiation for the thesis that private practice in social work originated as a psychotherapeutically oriented attempt to gain more autonomy while acquiring a middle-class clientele:

Our own attitude toward casework has changed. We no longer want to be a service for the "underprivileged." We are doing much creative thinking regarding the role of casework in the whole community. . . . What about the families who never come to clinics, agencies, courts? Have we really a service we should be offering them? And if so, how shall we offer it?[27]

Although Steiner believed that she had found the way to offer such a service, the economic difficulties of the time made the experiment short-lived. She listed finances as the major handicap making private practice impractical at the time and remarked that "had the venture not been undertaken during the Depression it might easily have succeeded financially as well as professionally."[28]

Given the apparent open-mindedness of psychiatric social work toward private practice during the 1920s and 1930s, it seems likely that the decline of the middle class during the Great Depression had more to do with the decline of interest in this approach than any need on the part of private practitioners to go underground, as some have suggested.[29] Reynolds and French each described the decline of opportunities for working relationships between psychiatrists and social workers as the result of the depression, as well as to the migration of psychiatric social workers to family service agencies where there was work administering temporary emergency relief funds.[30] French's study of trends in psychiatric social work during the 1920s and early 1930s provides additional support for this hypothesis. According to the survey of the AAPSW membership that she used for her analysis, a number of the association's members had been engaged in private psychiatric social work prior to 1930, but there was no evidence of further extension of this practice after 1930.[31]

AFTER THE WAR: PRIVATE PRACTICE GAINS ACCEPTANCE

During the period of economic expansion following World War II, the demand for social workers to work with psychiatrists in both inpatient and outpatient settings increased markedly as a result of the need for mental health treatment of returning veterans and the increasing appreciation for mental health services on the part of the middle class. Simultaneously, debate developed concerning the differences and similarities between the social casework performed by social workers and the psychotherapy performed by physicians and clinical psychologists. The terms of this debate reflected the dominance of psychoanalytic theory in both social work and psychiatry during the late 1940s and the 1950s.[32] Some members of both professions considered the differences to be largely "semantic" or quantitative rather than qualitative in nature.[33]

Often, when differences are delineated, a closer examination reveals differences in therapy technique rather than actual qualitative distinctions between casework and psychotherapy. For example, Florence Hollis, a professor of social work at Columbia University, defined the means by which social casework achieved its ends as "environmental modification," "psychological support," "clarification," and "insight development." She argued that the difference between the insight developed by social casework and that developed in psychoanalysis was one of depth, with social workers dealing with transference feelings but not with the transference neurosis, which was the analyst's exclusive turf.[34] The purpose of this quibbling about levels of consciousness was to mollify any fear physicians might have that social workers were encroaching on their territory. These discussions are echoed today in attempts to delineate the differences between psychoanalysis and psychoanalytic-psychotherapy.

Of course, some social workers and psychiatrists felt that a great difference did (or should) divide social casework and psychotherapy. The psychiatrists, no doubt unhappy with the upstart social workers treading on their turf, thought that the domain of social workers should be limited to "adjustment advisor with a goal of limited adjustment."[35] Some social workers saw a clear distinction between social casework and psychotherapy, arguing that individual personality change was never the goal of casework and that the purpose of any individual social caseworker could not be separated from the purpose of the agency for which she or he worked.[36] These social workers had remained true to, and had continued to develop, the earlier social work tradition, which sought to comprehend the client's difficulties from a social interaction perspective, placing primary emphasis on understanding the client's social relations. Ruth Smalley, a professor of social work at the University of Pittsburgh, articulated this other position in 1947:

The nature of the help offered by the social worker is *not* total personality change for the client or member as it is for the analyst. Social work has *its own purpose—that of helping the individual deal with problems in his social situation*—the nature of the problems and the kinds of services offered being determined by the purpose of the agency offering the services, with any personality change accruing as a by-product of services well offered through the methods of *social work,* which are different from the methods of psychoanalysis, diluted or straight.[37]

Those who saw a unique role for social work also conceived of the social service agency as both the source of sanction for the social caseworker's efforts as well as a representation of the collective reality and community from which the client comes for help and to which the client must ultimately return for help.[38] In fact, much of the later debate on the appropriateness of private practice in social work centered on whether a person practicing outside a social work agency was doing social work at all.

While the debate concerning social casework and psychotherapy continued from the late 1940s throughout the 1950s, albeit to a decreasing degree, there was also a renewed interest in private practice. In 1947, Rowena Ryerson and Elizabeth Weller, two social workers from New York, shared with the larger social work community their experiences in developing a private practice. In one year's time they had developed a full-time private practice, which they preferred to identify as "psychotherapy, feeling that this term covers a wide range of techniques." Almost all of their referrals came from psychiatrists and psychoanalysts practicing in the community, and they obtained psychiatric consultation on every case. Ryerson and Weller concluded that the demand for their service existed for two primary reasons. First, there was a group of "persons of adequate means who have always paid for private medical care" and also expected to pay on a private basis for psychotherapeutic services rendered as supplemental to psychiatric attention. These middle-class clients were considered unlikely to visit a social service agency because of the stigma attached. Second, certain clients were referred to the private practitioner because of a "lack of availability of psychiatric time" that at least some of the time coincided with a patient's inability or unwillingness to enter psychoanalysis. These patients would then be referred to the "psychotherapists" for a "less deep type of therapy."[39]

The methods Ryerson and Weller used in their practice came directly from their psychoanalytic training, perhaps tempered by their extensive experience working in psychiatric and family casework settings. However, whatever emphasis had been placed on external or environmental factors in their previous agency-based casework experience, they did not find these to be of great import in working with their new clients:

> The number of cases referred for a practical service on an environmental level has been minimal and . . . in almost every one of these cases emotional problems have interfered with the patient's ability to make use of this practical help without there first being some psychological help. Thus, although the original referral may have been made on the basis of environmental need, the focus of treatment shifted to a consideration of the emotional problem involved.[40]

In 1950, Josephine Peek and Charlotte Plotkin of the New York School of Social Work, Columbia University, reported the results of the first study of the growth of private practice in social casework after World War II. They noted that middle-class clients in the past had been deterred from seeking social casework services from private agencies because of the stigma associated with charity.[41] But during the 1940s, social service agencies had begun to establish fee-for-service programs for persons with emotional problems, partly in response to a decline in demand for concrete services from these agencies as a result of the growth of government public assistance programs. Peek and Plotkin associated this effort to provide services to the middle class with the even newer development of private social casework practice.

They confined their study to New York City, where they were able to complete thirty interviews with social workers in private practice. They believed this group to be the lion's share of private practitioners in New York. Their respondents were more highly educated than social workers generally, with twenty-seven having a master's degree and seven having begun or completed a doctoral program. The powerful allegiance of social caseworkers in that day to psychoanalytic theory is illustrated by the fact that eighteen of the respondents had attended seminars led by prominent psychoanalysts or psychiatrists and that all but three had either completed or entered into their own personal analysis.[42]

These private practitioners, like those to follow them, had extensive agency experience. Two-thirds had supervisory experience in agencies, and almost as many had held governing board positions in leading casework agencies. Most were members of the AAPSW, and more were members of the National Psychology Association for Psychoanalysis than of the American Association of Social Workers.[43]

When asked why they had entered private practice, the primary reasons given had to do with limitations imposed on their casework practice by agency policies, the incompatibility of agency schedules with family responsibilities, and the fact that they were made able to do so by support from psychiatrists, supervisors, and other colleagues. Increased income was also mentioned as an important factor contributing to the move to private practice.[44]

The growth of private practice, at least in New York City, seems clearly to have been a postwar phenomenon; twenty-six of the thirty respondents to the survey had entered private practice between 1945 and 1950, and only one had done so before 1943. This adds support to the hypothesis that economic constraints, rather than professional rejection, had undermined the growth of private practice after a hopeful beginning in the 1920s. It is no wonder that the momentum for private practice had been lost during the depression, given that it was clearly a service for the middle class. While the private practitioners felt that their fees were lower than those of analysts and psychiatrists, the practices of twenty-nine of the thirty caseworkers were made up primarily of middle-income clients; one practitioner saw only upper-income clients.[45]

These social caseworkers in private practice did not, for the most part, refer to themselves as social workers or to their practice as social work, preferring instead to describe their work using psychotherapeutic terminology. In general, they believed that schools of social work of that period did not provide them with the in-depth skills they believed to be necessary for private practice.[46]

There was considerable concern on the part of the private practitioners regarding the confusion surrounding the question of
who was in fact qualified to practice psychotherapy. Was an M.S.
degree in social work adequate? Did one need an M.D. or a Ph.D.
in psychology, and if so were these degrees proper credentials for
private practice? Should one be required to have a certain
amount of supervised experience prior to private practice, and
who is qualified to provide such supervision? The experience of
these early private practitioners led them to conclude that there
should be a universally required curriculum and set of licensing
standards for all persons seeking to practice psychotherapy privately, regardless of their professional affiliation.[47]

By the late 1950s, the profession finally took note of the growing private practice of social casework as well as the growing influence of advocates for private practice. In 1957, the National
Association of Social Workers' (NASW) Commission on Social
Work Practice developed a definition of social work private practice and proposed interim minimum standards, thereby suggesting that private practice was within the realm of professional social work. By 1964, the NASW had adopted minimum standards
for private practice and officially recognized it as a legitimate
area of social work, while affirming that "practice within socially
sponsored organizational structures must remain the primary
avenue for the implementation of the goals of the profession."[48]
During this time, governments also began to take notice by regulating and licensing the private practice of psychotherapy. California first passed a licensing law for social workers in 1945. In
1953, San Diego specifically required the licensing of social workers in private practice, and by 1965 California had enacted a law
requiring the licensing of practitioners of marriage, family, and
child counselors.[49] The pressure from professional social workers
and others who lay claim to the psychotherapy market has led to
a proliferation of regulation, licensing, and vendorship laws
across the country. Today, all of the states have some sort or recognized status for social workers in clinical practice, which
means, for the most part, the private practice of psychotherapy.[50]

Since there are few empirical studies of the private practice of
psychotherapy by social workers prior to the 1960s, we have had
to rely heavily on the voices of practitioners themselves as pre-

sented in the social work literature of the times to create a picture of the growth of social workers' interest in psychotherapy and private practice prior to formal acceptance by the profession. The outlines of this picture are clear. Some social workers adopted psychotherapeutic practice as a way of accomplishing a number of "professional" goals that seemed problematic in the context of the agencies in which they worked. They wanted more autonomy in their practice, including the authority to develop psychotherapeutic relationships with their clients, unhindered by agency constraints. In essence, the would-be private practitioners wanted to be their own bosses. Furthermore, they wanted access to "eager, thoughtful students of life." In less glowing terms, they wanted a middle-class clientele who might make better use of a psychotherapeutic service and who could help them to acquire the increased income that they desired.

Although the aspiration of many social workers to have their own private practice is consistent with developments in other professions, there is something quirky about this lust for autonomy and solo practice in a profession whose traditional foundation and ethos lies in its commitment to, and expertise in, the creation of social approaches to solving the problems of individuals and groups. Why is psychotherapy, an approach primarily oriented to individual solutions, practically the only service offered by social workers in private practice? What is this attraction of social workers to a middle-class clientele?

From the sociological perspective, the growth of private practice in social work can be seen as a "collective mobility project" of members of the middle class seeking to gain control over the provision of a valued service commodity.[51] This position has been forcefully argued by some within the social work profession who point to the potential conflicts between the social class interests of upwardly mobile social workers and those poor and working-class persons with whom they most often work in agency settings.[52] The private practice of psychotherapy provides a way to avoid those conflicts by avoiding the clients of a certain class who create those conflicts. To the extent that private practitioners make considerably more money than social workers in public and private agencies, it is also a way of accelerating one's climb up the economic ladder.

In the case of social work, however, the political-economic model of professionalization may not explain everything. The American ideology of expressive individualism seems to exercise a strong pull too. Psychotherapists, the secular priests of the modern era who have the task of guiding us in our monadic quest for a psychic home, have been given a great deal of prestige and economic privilege. It is the psychotherapists, not the social workers, who write the popular nonfiction of our era and appear on television and radio talk shows. Social workers, on the other hand, are charged with caring and advocating for those members of society toward whom society has had at best an ambivalent attitude. Social workers themselves are treated with that same public ambivalence at best, but more frequently with contempt for their practice. Furthermore, except when confronted by an external threat, Americans have a hard time finding faith in collective, communal, or social approaches to solving problems. We prefer to see failure, illness, incapacity, and, conversely, success as individually determined personal qualities. Even when we concede the presence of a contributing social or historic dynamic, such as economic recession or war, we either shrug our shoulders in an expression of resignation in the face of such social forces or, more commonly, call to mind one of the myriad success stories at our conscious disposal that reassures us that the individual does have the ability to make it against all odds. It is no wonder that social work, which inevitably confronts its practitioners with disquieting social phenomena that belie the expressive individualist myth and occasionally succeeds in confronting the general public with the same news, has been granted low status by society and has seen many of its best opt for a redefinition of their professional role into something more socially and financially rewarding and palatable.

Nevertheless, there have long been those who have argued that if the search for a more respectable and independent professional role for social workers leads away from the public and private agency social services and into an allegiance with the ideology of individualism, then that search will have found at its end the ruins of a great tradition of social reform and social care that was social work. Dr. Jules Coleman of the University of Colorado Medical School in 1947 suggested that social casework involved a more "far-reaching respect of person than is found in psychiatry, or, for that matter, medicine and lamented the worship of psychotherapy by caseworkers:

> The caseworker has good reason to be beguiled by the lures of psychotherapy, to seize upon the points of similarity and to skim lightly over the gulfs of difference, particularly if the practice of psychotherapy is unwisely and unthinkingly accorded undue prestige values. As if the practice of casework did not suffice! As if doing psychotherapy made the caseworker a better and more valuable person![53]

In the same year, long before the private practice of psychotherapy would become a major trend in social work practice, Ruth Smalley expressed the fears of many in the field regarding the fascination with psychotherapy: "A blight which is in danger of falling on the profession of social work is a lack of confidence and respect for itself. It is almost as though it thinks that it can find dignity, status, and helpfulness only by becoming something it is not."[54]

PSYCHOTHERAPY AND SOCIAL WORK TODAY

A common theme of private practice advocates within the social work profession recently has been that the debate over private practice should be considered moot. The NASW has accepted private practice as a valid method of social work practice; thousands of social workers are already practicing psychotherapy privately under the protection of regulation and vendorship laws won only after tough battles fought by the social work profession against other competing mental health professions; thousands of middle-class clients have demonstrated their support for social work private practice by paying for it out of their own pockets. Why continue this divisive debate that should have ended forty years ago?

We acknowledge that all of these developments and more have occurred as a result of the success of social work private practice. However, a close examination of the magnitude of that practice, what it consists of, and the direction in which it is leading the profession forces us to conclude that the debate must be rejoined with more fervor than ever.

The private practice of psychotherapy by social workers has gained a position in the social work labor market that even its advocates may be reluctant to admit. From a handful of psychiatric social workers in the 1920s, private practice has grown into what social work labor scholar David Hardcastle calls "the most obvious and significant trend in the social work labor market."[55] Between 1975 and 1985, the number of social workers in full-time private practice increased more than fivefold, and more than one-third of the NASW membership in 1985 engaged in private practice.[56] A study done for the California chapter of NASW found that approximately 30 percent of employed NASW members were employed in private for-profit settings and that psychotherapy is the primary practice method employed by about 39 percent of all members.[57] No study to date has considered the number of individuals, educated and trained as social workers, who enter private practice but do not affiliate themselves with one of the professional associations. Given the reluctance over the years for social workers who practice psychotherapy to acknowledge an allegiance to social work, there is good reason to take a conservative view of these estimates.

The growth in private practice coincides with the development of mental health as the primary professional base of social work, with 29 percent of the social work labor force employed in mental health settings, nearly twice as many as in any other practice area. In fact, social work is the single largest mental health profession, accounting for about 38 percent of the professional personnel in the field.[58]

There is every reason to believe that these trends will continue. The U.S. Bureau of Labor Statistics projects employment of social workers in mental health counseling positions in both agency and private practice to grow rapidly through the year 2000.[59] Recent studies indicate that between one-fifth and one-third of incoming M.S.W. students ultimately plan to have full-time private practice careers.[60] Furthermore, although these students express a desire to work with at least one of the disadvantaged groups traditionally associated with social work practice (e.g., the chronically mentally disabled or the frail aged), these groups have much less appeal than do clients with nonchronic psychological problems (e.g., college students in emotional crisis or couples having marital difficulties), who are the type of clients that make up the average private psychotherapy practice. These incoming students also find psychotherapeutic techniques to be the practice methods with the most appeal.[61]

Studies have revealed the following characteristics of social work private practitioners and their practices:

- Private practitioners are significantly more likely to be Caucasian than either social workers in general or the clients they see in their practices.
- Social workers in private practice earn significantly better incomes on average than public or private agency social workers.
- Private practitioners, more often than not, have obtained additional clinical education beyond their M.S.W.
- Private practice is truly private for the practitioner to the extent that social workers in private practice are twice as likely to work solo as in a group practice with other colleagues.
- Private practitioners are more involved in social work professional organizations than other social workers.
- Almost all private practitioners refer to what they do as "psychotherapy," while only about half identify themselves in their practice as social workers.
- The clients seen by private practitioners are almost exclusively middle class.
- Private practitioners work primarily with persons exhibiting nonchronic psychological problems, thus leaving the chronically mentally ill and severely disturbed to go elsewhere.[62]

Social workers enter private practice today for the same reasons that they have been attracted to the private practice of psychotherapy since the 1920s: to obtain more autonomy over their practice and to earn more money.[63] The findings of a recent study of the goals of private practitioners in New England upon entering private practice bring the priorities of these social workers into stark relief. The most important goals indicated by the survey respondents, in decreasing order of importance, were to "do direct counseling, "maximize professional autonomy," "grow professionally," "be my own boss," "set my own hours,"and "earn money." The least important goals indicated, in decreasing order of importance, were "help solve society's problem," "become more politically involved," "help economically disadvantaged people," and "work with ethnic minorities." It is important to note that these people had been well socialized into the social work profession; they had an average of ten years of post-M.S.W. social work experience prior to entering private practice.[64]

Another position that advocates of private practice and others within the mental health wing of social work sometimes take is that clinical social work provides a unique service that focuses on the relationship between the client and his or her environment in a way that is absent in the clinical approaches of other mental health professions.[65] If this were the case, there might be a valid argument for defining and protecting a separate mental health professional status for clinical social workers. However, as social work philosopher Jerome Wakefield has noted: "A quick glance at a variety of professional journals inside and outside of social work will dispel the idea. Social work does not have a monopoly on an interactional or social approach to mental disorder, and many social workers do not actually work in this way."[66] Our review of the mental health literature agrees with Wakefield's.

Empirical evidence also contradicts the notion that clinical social workers offer a unique service among the mental health professions. A study of the practice of NASW-affiliated clinical social workers during the late 1970s indicated that they were wide ranging in their descriptions of the theoretical views that informed their practice. The percentages indicating the use of different theories in their practice were as follows: psychoanalytic, 53 percent; reality therapy, 47.7 percent; humanistic, 41.7 percent; neo-Freudian, 32.7 percent; behavior therapy, 32.3 percent; gestalt, 27.8 percent; Rogerian, 21.2 percent; existential, 20.7 percent; transactional analysis, 20.3 percent; rational emotive, 11.3 percent; and other, 17.7 percent.[67] One would be hard-pressed to find a unifying social work perspective among these responses.

A more recent study of private mental health practitioners in Maryland compared the preferred theoretical orientations of social workers, psychiatrists, psychologists, and nurses. The findings illustrate the lack of a clear distinction between the approaches of clinical social work and these other professions. Moreover, although some differences in degree were distinguishable, no distinctive preference pattern emerged for any profession.[68] Similarly, a review of the psychotherapy outcome literature comparing the therapeutic orientations and methods of psychiatrists, psychologists, and social workers as well as the effectiveness of the therapy provided by these professions concluded that "professional affiliation predicts neither therapeutic activities nor outcome."[69] It seems that the robes of the secular priests and priestesses of our era are all cut from the same cloth.

This should not be surprising. Over twenty years ago, a sociological study was undertaken of psychoanalysts, psychiatrists, clinical psychologists, and psychiatric social workers in New York, Chicago, and Los Angeles. The researchers found that these clinicians have more in common with each other with respect to culture, religion, politics, and social class than they do with other members of their respective professions. Furthermore, in spite of the differing professional training paths followed by these mental health practitioners, the completion of their professional evolution seems to bring them all to the same point. These results prompted the authors to question the social economy of retaining four different training systems to produce essentially the same professional: the psychotherapist. They called for the creation of a fifth profession.[70] Agreement with this position comes from a surprising source: social workers in private practice. In a survey of NASW members in private practice conducted in 1976, 63 percent of the respondents indicated that they favored the merging of the clinical wings of the mental health professions into a single profession of psychotherapy.[71]

IT'S TIME TO MOVE ON

We hold no particular brief against psychotherapy and psychotherapists per se; they serve an important social function. We also
readily acknowledge that psychotherapeutic techniques play a
role in many valid social work interventions that are properly
within the realm of social work's function. However, it is one
thing to borrow the techniques of others in order to improve the
service offered by one's profession and quite another to forget
the mission of one's profession.[72] Social work is in a position to
become little more than another mental health profession. With
its ongoing neglect of the public social services, it seems ready to
embrace as its primary function what was once considered pe-
ripheral.

Although social work psychotherapists can lay no claim to a
unique and invaluable approach to mental health treatment, this
has not stopped them from exerting considerable influence
within and without the profession toward creating special recognition of their practice. In fact, it is arguable that the growing influence of private practitioners within the profession has contributed to the tendency of the profession over the past twenty years
to use more of its political clout to push for licensure and vendorship privileges for clinicians than for services to the needy or for
better working conditions for public agency social workers. A
study by Timothy Lause of the number-one legislative priorities
of NASW state chapters during the late 1970s indicates that two-
thirds of these priorities concerned licensure or third-party payments, while only one-third had to do with social problem-
solving policies and services. Lause found that even in states
where there was already some regulation of the profession (and,
therefore, presumably more room to be concerned about other
social programs and policies), the legislative emphasis shifted
more toward third-party payments than toward social problems
and services.[73] The more recent focus upon vendorship issues of
the 1984 NASW Delegate Assembly and the 1985–1986 NASW
lobbying program indicate similar developments at the national
level.[74]

Nor is the battle for psychotherapeutic privilege likely to be over very soon. With soaring health costs causing insurance providers and health maintenance organizations to limit mental health services, we can be sure that the cries of "our therapy is better than your therapy" from the competing psychotherapy camps will be louder than ever.[75] In fact, with the psychopharmacological approaches of psychiatry and brief/behavioral approaches of psychology potentially appearing less expensive to insurers and the government, social workers in private practice may be scrambling again to maintain their ground, draining even more of the profession's limited political and social clout away from the needs of the employees and users of the public social services into profession building for psychotherapists.

It is time for the social workers to abandon their fascination with psychotherapy and reinvest themselves in the important process of developing and improving their profession.

CHAPTER SIX

SOCIAL WORK IN THE TWENTY-FIRST CENTURY

Replacing Psychotherapy with Community Education

◆◆◆◆

We have an alternative vision of a program for a profession that is truly committed to the great twenty-first-century social mission of establishing community-based social care in the United States. In order to carry out this mission, social work must discard the psychotherapeutic model of clinical practice that a majority of social workers have used for decades and in its place develop a new practice model that is based on an adult education approach to problem solving. Before we sketch out a model of practice, some theoretical and philosophical issues must be resolved. We focus on these in this chapter.

AMERICAN PREFERENCES FOR INDIVIDUAL SOLUTIONS TO SOCIAL PROBLEMS

Many Americans fail to understand that a number of the problems we experience as individuals can be dealt with most effectively when they are perceived to be social problems that require social solutions.[1] For example, many of the lonely, frail, and demented aged are *our* aged parents and the parents of our friends, employees, and relatives. And, of course, many of us are the lonely, frail, and demented aged of the future. How the community deals with the problems of the aged will affect the quality of all of our lives at some time. Yet large numbers of Americans prefer not to see how this and related problems affect us now or to know how they will affect us in the future.

Generations of Americans have been brainwashed with psychological and psychiatric theories that identify the individual as the source of many problems that are basically social in origin. From early childhood, Americans are socialized and educated to believe that with proper attitudes, insight, behavioral training, and motivation, the individual can overcome almost any social problem: child abuse, depression, loneliness, anomie, chemical abuse, and others. Thus, Americans of all social classes—poor and rich alike—have a trained incapacity to see the community as either the cause or the solution of social problems.

Social welfare policy and social work practice are closely related. Family and community policy is eventually seen in the ways that professionals and public institutions go about helping people and, especially, in the extent to which methods, procedures, and policies support the resources of families and communities to help themselves.

That there are contradictions in governmental social policy on the family and community has been well documented.[2] The implementers of social policies cannot help but be socialized into the values of the systems in which they work. The success of this socialization is enhanced by the screening of prospective professionals into professional schools and the socialization that takes place in professional education, which is followed by the screening of these professionals into social welfare bureaucracies.

The most significant values that American professionals carry into their work are individualism and expertise. These values are mutually supporting. Expertise is the sine qua non of the professional.[3] The claim professionals make to the perquisites and privileges of their positions rests on the belief (which may or may not correspond to fact) that only the professional intervener is capable of helping the service user. Pruger and Specht have stated:

> The professional imagination has much to recommend it. It permits those who are to be helped to spurn the help offered without any weakening of the professional's desire to help; it returns disciplined understanding for impulsive rancor; it demands hard

working conditions. Indeed, it embodies the finest in civilized behavior, holding nothing in the human experience foreign to it,
save one—the notion that the helped, except in certain prescribed,
professionally approved ways, can or should be the helpers.[4]

One would not expect that human services professions would
find it difficult to incorporate the notion that major resources for
helping lie not only with the professional but also with the service user and his or her family and community. However, the
value placed on individualism in American life frequently con-
strains a professional from enabling service users to maximize
their own resources. This preference for working with individuals occurs for several reasons. First, most professionals are of
middle-class origin. Those who are from working-class backgrounds become socialized to middle-class values, which, often,
they embrace with even greater fervor than those who were born
into them.[5] Therefore, many professionals may denigrate the life-
styles and values of lower-class service users. In the context of
this discussion, these value differences may result in professionals' setting greater value on individual achievement, initiative, and independence than on more communalistic and non-
competitive behaviors.

Second, a majority of human service professionals work in bureaucratic systems, which for the most part are not organized to
deal with clients as groups or as members of groups, whether in
family units, extended kinship systems, or community groups.[6]
Bronfenbrenner put it succinctly:

That the family is the core institution in every society may startle
and annoy many contemporary Americans. For most of us it is the
individual that is the chief social unit. We speak of the *individual* vs.
the state, *individual* achievement, support for disadvantaged *individuals*, the rights of *individuals*, finding ourselves as *individuals*.
It's always the *individual* with "the government" a weak second.
The family is not currently a social unit we value or support.[7]

Third, most professionals receive their education and are socialized into the human services professions at a time of life when
they themselves are disengaged from their families and communities of origin, have not yet started their own families, and do

not live in communities populated overwhelmingly by families. They are emotionally and socially divorced from the major concerns of family and community life. Moreover, all schools of social work in the United States have one or more required courses on human development that usually focus on the development of the individual through the life cycle but no required course on the family and community.

Over the past two decades, there has been more social acceptance of a wider variety of social relationships—for example, homosexual couples, single-parent families, and communal living—and a wider range of social roles for both men and women. At the same time, insufficient attention is given to the need for finding new ways to establish social commitment, communality, and caring. Rather, the concern is with self-realization and self-expression; these are, in our view, only popular expressions of individualism.[8]

THE VARYING SOCIAL UTILITY OF DIFFERENT MODES OF INTERVENTION

The evidence to support the efficacy of individual psychotherapy for dealing with social problems is extremely weak. Even as a solution for problems of individuals, research on the effectiveness of psychotherapy indicates that all brands and types of psychotherapy tend to produce about the same results. In a substantial review of this research, Stiles, Shapiro, and Elliot comment as follows:

> Despite the plethora of purportedly distinct psychotherapeutic treatments, influential reviews of comparative outcome research together with frequently cited studies appear to support the conclusion that outcomes of diverse therapies are generally similar. Efforts to base public policy recommendations concerning mental health care service provisions on scientific evidence have yielded only "a consensus, of sorts, . . . on the question of the efficacy of psychotherapy as a generic treatment process . . . that psychotherapy is more effective than no treatment." No such consensus exists concerning the relative effectiveness of diverse therapies. The

verdict of the Dodo bird in *Alice's Adventures in Wonderland*, . . . "Everybody has won and all must have prizes," captures this situation most vividly.[9]

If all types of psychotherapeutic interventions produce about the same results, it would make sense to favor one or another kind of intervention on two grounds: the degree of efficiency of the intervention and the social utility of the intervention.

First, let us consider the factor of efficiency. If, for example, the same results can be achieved in one to three counseling sessions with therapist A who is committed to brief, time-limited treatment as can be achieved in one to three years of psychoanalysis with therapist B, it would seem clear that, all other things being equal, therapist A would be the obvious choice. Moshe Talmon has both reviewed the literature on this subject and carried out his own research. He found a great deal of evidence that a majority of patients attain what they want from a single interview with a psychotherapist and that this occurs regardless of the therapist's theoretical approach or style. Most therapists, however, will report those who do not show up for a second interview as "dropouts" and explain their behavior in such terms as "resistance," "borderline personality," and "lacking motivation for change."[10] Clearly, it would require a major overhaul in a therapist's perception of and appreciation of a service user's own social and emotional resources and capacities to accept the idea that most people do not have to become dependent on a therapist to deal with problems of living.

Many clients seek drawn-out treatments—perhaps because of ignorance; because longer, more protracted treatments have the appearance of being more potent; because they like and feel good about their therapists and their therapy; or because therapists themselves prescribe longer interventions because longer is in their own self-interest. Whatever the reason is, therapists and their patients cannot be relied upon to select the most efficient means of intervention.[11]

Frequently, it is the insurance companies or other health-providing organizations that pay the bills that set limits on the number of therapeutic sessions per client for which they are willing to pay. If users are willing to pay for treatment out of their own pockets, they are entitled to purchase the treatment of their choice within the bounds of safety and honesty established by licensing laws. However, if the treatments are to be paid for by all of us, through the tax system or insurance programs, then policy-makers must assume responsibility for establishing policies and guidelines for what seem to be the most practical and socially useful interventions on which to spend public money.

The second factor that should enter into the calculation in the selection of interventions is their degree of social utility. Interventions that are effective for individuals will be of varying utility to the community; an individual may like a particular kind of treatment, but its social value may be nil. For example, psychotherapy is variably effective for reducing child abuse.[12] However, communally based interventions to prevent child abuse—child care programs, for example—are socially useful whether or not they result in less destructive behavior on the part of any particular individual. The availability of child care programs ensures that children are placed in a physically safe and healthy environment in the absence of their parents and that they are provided with educational and stimulating experiences and improved nutrition. In addition, parents who use child care programs have strong incentives, social supports, and positive role models for learning parenting skills. They have, too, strong disincentives against abusing and neglecting their children because such behavior is likely to be observed, disapproved of, and reported by staff members and other parents involved in the child care programs.

Thus, programs of social care constitute strong preventative measures to deal with many social problems such as child abuse, loneliness, and the mentally ill. But what about victims of such problems: abused and neglected children or the spouses and children of alcoholics? Ought not therapeutic treatment be available to them? Perhaps. But the question of which treatments are most efficacious and therapeutic remains. The evidence supporting the utility of radical individual therapies is not strong. And the evidence supporting the social and psychological utility of more communalistic types of interventions to deal with problems experienced by individuals is at least as strong. The benefits to society of communalistic modes of intervention provide a compelling argument for them.

RECOGNIZING THE CENTRALITY
OF THE INDIVIDUAL

The most serious criticism psychotherapists may make is that we give insufficient attention to the individual. Paul Saxton, one of California's foremost social work private practitioners of psychotherapy, has said of our approach to practice that it is not based on knowledge

> of the realities of contemporary clinical social work, defined as "interventions focused on individuals, families, and small groups." Informed by the advances in understanding of the psyche and its relationships to its world, clinicians in any setting respond to clients with a variety of techniques based on their professional assessment of clients' needs. . . . And to suggest that all poor people need is community building is to add to their disadvantage by depriving them of their unconscious. The private practitioner, particularly in today's managed care environment, often provides short-term ego-building "developmental socialization" in the tasks of daily living to poorly functioning clients, while the competent child welfare worker assists parents and children to move beyond the wounds of earlier dysfunction to increased competence in social role performance. . . . The distinctions [made between psychotherapy and social work] are dangerous to clients and wildly unrealistic as definitions of professional boundaries.[13]

Saxton is concerned that in a community-oriented system, the poor might not get their fair share of psychotherapy—a modern-day version of letting them eat cake. Not only does he think that in opposing psychotherapeutic practice in social work we are "depriving the poor of their unconscious," he says that psychotherapy "is not about problem solving and coping." It is, rather, he says, " a grindingly painful struggle for transformation and birth of the self. . . . [It is] about confrontations with the demons within and without."[14]

Some professionals will criticize our approach to practice on the claim that we neglect the individual. The fact is that we believe that the well-educated professional social worker must have a high level of knowledge about human growth and development, psychological and behavioral social problems, and the dynamics and processes of social interaction. There are, in fact, many similarities and significant overlap in the knowledge used by social workers and psychotherapists.[15] But it is not sources of knowledge that distinguish one profession from another. Rather, it is the way in which a profession integrates and uses knowledge to carry out a particular mission that marks it as distinct.

Social workers use knowledge about human development and behavior in order to determine the kinds of help people need. Social groups, educational classes, community organizations, and other sorts of associations are, after all, composed of individuals. If social workers are to develop and strengthen communally supported services they must begin by assessing the problems, needs, resources, and strengths of the persons who will be involved in these collectivities. This includes a capacity to understand the developmental, intellectual, emotional, and social needs of persons, taking into account, too, the ways their needs are affected by gender, race, ethnicity, and religion, social class, and sexual orientation.

It is necessary, though, to distinguish between the importance of knowledge about individual development and the choice of a social intervention. That is, to say that concern for individuals and their needs is central to the professional social worker's way of thinking is not to say that the best program for solving problems will be to work with individuals one by one.

The ways in which social work professionals respond to the problems that service users bring to them is influenced considerably by the theoretical perspectives they have about human development. For example, professionals who are orthodox Freudians tend to explain their client's problems as manifestations of unconscious conflicts about how to meet instinctual needs; professionals who are Marxists usually find ways to explain how the economic system causes the problems their clients experience.

This tendency was illustrated in a recent research report on how social workers perceived clients' problems. Rosen and Livne found that, in comparison to a panel of experts, social workers identified personal problems more frequently than environmental problems when they analyzed a case record. Moreover, they found that this tendency on the part of the social workers was positively related to their having a psychodynamic orientation about human development and negatively related to their using a concrete approach in provision of practical help and support.[16]

There are two major ways in which human development is viewed by the social sciences. The more popular view tends to support a one-by-one approach to problem solution. We refer to this as the individualist view of human development. The major alternative view can be referred to as the collectivist view.

The individualist view of human behavior relies primarily on an understanding of the dynamics of the self and seldom ventures very far from that view. In general, from the individualist perspective the technology by which corrective changes occur is the talk that takes place between patient and psychotherapist. These talks take place more or less frequently (depending on how "sick" or "resistant" the patient is believed to be and how much money is available for the treatment), with the therapist doing varying amounts of the talking.

The major instrument used in this treatment is the therapist. It is the therapist's ability to understand and manage a relationship with a patient that is key. Management of the patient-therapist relationship is not an easy business. But when the relationship is well managed, it is the therapist, and only the therapist, who is in charge of the treatment. The patient remains dependent upon the therapist. The patient, who is extremely vulnerable to begin with, is often mystified and confused by the complex technology of the proceedings and may be kept uninformed about what is taking place.

An alternative view of human development tends to support a more communalistic approach to the solution of social problems. We refer to this perspective as the collectivist view of human development. With this view, the process of human development is perceived to be one in which individuals learn to become participants in the organized social life around them—the family, neighborhood, school, work, voluntary associations, government, and so on.[17] The focus of attention is not the individual but, rather, the process by which individuals participate in and utilize collective life.

In the collectivist view, human growth and development is not a serial process that starts with birth and ends in old age and death. There is good evidence that the process of human development occurs over and over again throughout the life cycle, and each time it occurs, it opens up new possibilities for growth and change.[18] The process is a recapitulation of the kind of collective experiences that have been written about in the literature on social movements, collective behavior, and different methods of working with groups.[19] People often refer to themselves as being "born again"; patients in hospitals, new recruits to the military, and people in summer camps, prisons, schools, monasteries, and self-help groups write similarly of the process of self-discovery and the achievement of new identities that occur at all ages.

The collectivist view of the process of human development is one in which a collectivity moves from being a disorganized aggregate, to discovering their need to depend on one another, to finding leadership, to establishing a corporate body, and finally, to becoming part of the transcendent institutional order.[20] This process of collective development—the recapitulation of the process of building a social entity—is quite different from the reliving of past experiences as occurs in Freud's transference relationships and in what he referred to as "the return of the repressed." In the collectivist view, people always enter the experience of collective development anew, finding themselves in situations that are different from past ones, with constellations of people who are different from past constellations of people they have known. There is in each experience the potential for new integrations of the selves of the participants and for new kinds of relationships to develop.

With the collectivist perspective, people are perceived to have the capacity to grow and change throughout the life cycle, creating new selves as they engage in new experiences. Individuals change over the course of their years, physically, intellectually, socially, and emotionally. As they enter new social experiences and interact with others—in college, courtship, on a job, or joining a social group or a political movement—they are in some ways different than they had been at earlier stages. The individual recapitulates the collective development experiences we describe. He or she comes to the new class, or the new job, or the new group feeling disconnected and uncertain about whether he or she belongs there and will fit in, but at a point he or she decides to throw in with the others and accepts interdependence. This person next discovers that he or she must cooperate with the others if the experience is to work. Study groups are formed, the larger group splits up into committees, and resources are shared. Following this, one or more members of the group takes the initiative in working out plans and coordinating everyone's efforts. The experience may continue through all of the stages of mentioned.

Collective development can stop at any stage. In the significant experiences of our lives, such as the establishment of a new family, or a new political party, or a new business, the collectivity may go on to establish an institutionalized transcendent order; arrangements can develop that permit for the replacement of social role incumbents who leave the collectivity so that it may continue to exist in perpetuity.

With aging, many people find it increasingly difficult to recapitulate the adjustment to new social contexts, a serious problem for the aging person because living organisms that cannot adjust to changing contextual conditions cannot survive.[21]

Thus, the collectivist view of human development focuses attention not on an individual client or service user but on the collectivity—on what is taking place between the professional and the service users and among the service users. It is the interpersonal interactions that occur among all of the participants in a social event that is of primary significance, rather than the intrapersonal experiences of an individual.

Individualist and collectivist theories about human behavior are neither entirely wrong nor entirely right. Each perspective illuminates certain facets of reality. Rather, the question is which theory is more useful for a particular purpose.

The major objective of practitioners of psychotherapy is to change the ways in which an individual feels about and perceives his or her own self. Individualistic theories will be most useful for this purpose because they focus attention on the internal experiences—the self—of the individual and the processes by which the self develops. The social work practitioner's objective, in our view, is to enable participants in groups, associations, organizations, and communities to deal with one another more effectively and to help individuals make best use of social resources. Collectivist types of theory are most useful for these purposes because they focus attention on groups and the social context rather than on the individual.

In reality, human experience is a mixture of the individual and the collective. Some ascribed human characteristics—examples are gender, race, height, and intelligence—are fixed. Other characteristics—such as social role, social class, social behavior, and attitudes and values—are relatively flexible and open. The possibilities of what can be done with both the relatively fixed and the relatively flexible traits as individuals enter new social contexts are extensive. The major technology through which this occurs is the activity of the group: discussions, planning, work, and recreational activities such as play, games, dancing, and dramatics. The major instrument used in this activity is the collectivity. The social worker's function is to facilitate the process by which the collectivity can achieve its goals. The goals of the collectivity will affect individual participants in different ways.

CHOOSING FROM A VARIETY OF INTERVENTIONS

Clinically oriented social workers have their criteria for selecting interventions backward. Common sense would suggest that we ought to use the quickest, easiest, and least expensive kinds of interventions before others. Yet clinical social workers usually begin with the most expensive and complex form of treatment—psychotherapy. Nevertheless, there is a range of interventions for social problems, described best as behavioral, normative, and personality interventions.[22]

The methods used in these different kinds of interventions vary. Behavioral interventions utilize training, education, modeling, instruction, and other means of imparting information and skills. They can be used on both an individual or group basis. Probably education and instruction in a group will provide social reinforcement and support to participants.

Normative interventions utilize coaching, advising, and a wide range of group activities, including discussions, debates, planning, public meetings, workshops, recreation, games, dance, and dramatics. Norms are learned in groups. The values, beliefs, and attitudes of individuals reflect the values, beliefs, and attitudes of the groups, both past and present, of which they are a part. For adults, some groups from the past are the family of origin and the adolescent peer group; some groups from the present are the work group, friends, relations, neighbors, and membership groups. An essential assumption of both behavioral and normative interventions is that problems of individuals are often the result of inadequate or dysfunctional normalizing processes in the social environment.

Finally, methods used for personality intervention are usually applied on a one-to-one basis: psychotherapy and tranquilizing drugs. Some psychotherapists use group methods as a means to change the perceptions that each individual member has of his or her self. Generally, the purpose is not to change the relationships that members have with one another or to increase the group's capacity to act on its own behalf.

The simplest and least expensive solution to a social problem is behavioral intervention. For example, one of our colleagues, Mr. Z, told us of his dealings with a young adult, Jack, who seemed anxious and tense. Jack was new to the city, lived by himself, and felt terribly lonely. He was having thoughts about suicide because he did not think he had the social ability or the physical looks to meet anyone. These feelings were all new to him, and he found his predicament to be very embarrassing. He did not know of anyone to whom he could talk about this.

After hearing about his concerns, Mr. Z. asked Jack how he had gone about meeting other young people. It turned out that he had not gone about it at all. He worked very long hours, although he did not have to, and he was then too tired to do anything else.

Mr. Z. talked with Jack about how some young adults meet— in singles' bars, at dances and meetings—and about how one finds out about these places to meet by asking friends, neighbors, and co-workers and by reading the newspapers. Jack showed great interest in this line of thought, and Mr. Z. asked Jack how he thought he would manage such encounters. Although Jack seemed to be somewhat shy, it sounded to Mr. Z. as if Jack could deal with such situations. Mr. Z. recommended that Jack read *Taking Charge of Your Social Life*, by Eileen Gambrill and Cheryl Richey.[23] Jack said he might try some of these ideas, and Mr. Z. made an appointment to see him again in two weeks.

At their second and last meeting, it was clear that Jack had begun to use Mr. Z.'s suggestions. He had gotten around to various places and events where he met some other young adults. He found the ideas in the book helpful. He was excited about what he had done and was confident that things would be better for him. Mr. Z. expressed pleasure at how well Jack was doing. There seemed no need for further contact, but Mr. Z. told Jack to call him at any time that he felt he needed to talk again.

In this case, behavioral intervention was clearly effective. Jack was able to make use of information and suggestions about how to solve his problems. It is not unlikely that he may even have known much of what Mr. Z. told him, and it was Mr. Z.'s warm, supportive, and friendly manner that gave Jack sufficient encouragement to make use of the knowledge.

Many self-help books that are sold popularly provide behavioral assistance of this sort. *How to Win Friends and Influence People* by Dale Carnegie is a classic example of a self-help book that is focused on behavior, as is Gambrill and Richey's book.[24]

In addition to being a simple and inexpensive kind of intervention, behavioral methods are helpful in a diagnostic way, too. Suppose Jack had said to Mr. Z. that he would never go to a singles' bar because he thought all people who did are sinful or diseased and that he would be in physical danger if he did go to such a place? This kind of response would suggest that Jack might have a more difficult problem to deal with than could be managed by behavioral interventions. Certainly, Mr. Z. ought to talk a little more with this young man.

But even with his response about sin and perdition, Mr. Z. ought not to rush Jack off to an institution or into intensive psychotherapy too quickly. Further exploration is called for. Mr. Z.

would want to have more information about Jack's background
and upbringing. Possibly the family and community norms—the
values, beliefs, and attitudes one learns in one's family, peer
group, and community—that Jack brought with him to the city
are causing him problems. It would help to know a bit more
about Jack's ethnic and religious affiliations. Perhaps normative
interventions would be helpful to Jack, such as referring him to a
community center, or church, or association run by his particular
ethnic or religious group.

If it turns out that Jack has a deep-seated problem—an illness—that prevents him from making use of either behavioral or
normative interventions, a personality kind of intervention
might be in order. More would have to be known of the nature
of Jack's illness in order to determine whether the best intervention would be drugs or psychotherapy or some kind of well-
structured social therapy, such as a group home, halfway house,
or sheltered workshop. The clinician would have to know, for example, whether the illness had an organic base or was caused by
an emotional or thinking disorder. Whatever the case, the professional ought not to consider using these more intrusive and expensive personality interventions without being completely persuaded that behavioral and normative interventions are not
feasible.

Many problems confronted by individuals are, by their very
nature, social problems. As we suggested in chapter 2, it is a great
leap of imagination to view the problems facing our hypothetical
woman who wants to regain custody of her children as personal.
A number of interventions, none resembling one-on-one psychotherapy, might be helpful to this woman. Arranging for child
care or even short-term respite care might have reduced the danger of abuse or neglect of the children enough to avoid the need
for out-of-home placement. Referral to a substance abuse treatment program, a self-help group for substance abusers, or some
other community-support activity may help the woman to stabilize her situation enough to avoid losing her children. Similar
supportive interventions prior to the breakup of the couple
might have helped to keep the nuclear family intact. In fact, since
the husband's layoff precipitated the deterioration in the family's
situation, community planning and social action to prevent the

plant closure and to provide job retraining for laid-off workers could have saved this family and many others.

Theoretically, one would expect that social work professionals would choose one-to-one interventions only as a last resort. Social interventions through classes, groups, voluntary associations, and community groups would seem to be the most desirable methods of intervention on all grounds: effectiveness, efficiency, and social utility. But unfortunately, it is the case in practice that psychotherapy is the treatment of choice for almost all problems.

THE GROUP AS THE MEDIUM OF CHOICE FOR SOCIAL WORK PRACTICE

One of the long-standing and recurrent findings from social psychological research is that the most effective way to change people's behavior is to change the norms of the groups of which they are members. For example, one of the best-known and most consistent findings in social psychological research is referred to as "the risky-shift" phenomenon. Social psychology made its major strides in this century during World War II, in research done for the military. In one major project, researchers were interested in ways to affect the choices for flying assignments made by air force bomber pilots. The researchers' major finding was that when the pilots made their decisions after a group discussion, the group's choices would shift; in a group, following a discussion, the pilots tended to select assignments that entailed more risk than they had selected when polled individually before the discussion; hence, the name "risky shift."[25] The meaning of the shifts was clarified by subsequent research over many years. Group discussion does not necessarily shift decisions in any particular direction—that is, to the more or the less "risky." Rather, discussion tends to shift decisions in the direction of the uncrystallized views of the majority of the group.[26]

Moreover, group decisions can be influenced in significant ways by the introduction of members who present differing beliefs and attitudes. For example, a group member who is alone in dissenting is likely to be ignored by, to become alienated from, or to be changed by the group. When just one more dissenter appears in the group, the choices, attitudes, and behavior of the group are more likely to shift. Interestingly, the additional dissenter does not have to agree with the first dissenter. The simple presence of more than one person with a different view appears to have a dramatic destabilizing effect upon group norms.[27] Such findings suggest that groups have the capacity to strengthen social change processes.

In another significant piece of wartime research, Kurt Lewin found that housewives were more likely to use unpopular cuts of meat, such as kidneys, if they participated in a discussion following a lecture than if they had only a lecture.[28] They found an even more dramatic change if the discussion following the lecture culminated in the participants' voting on what they would do in the future. This was some of the earliest research on the influence of member participation on behavior.

Psychotherapists are often reluctant to acknowledge the success of self-help groups, most likely because most such organizations expressly choose not to use professionals. If these groups were to become dependent on a professional for help and direction (as patients in psychotherapy must), then the "self" part of the idea of self-help would be diminished considerably.

Left-wing policymakers tend to dismiss self-help as government's way of shrugging off problems, while right-wing policymakers tend to embrace self-help as a way of shrugging off problems. Each position is somewhat correct. The most successful and enduring self-help groups involve a personal physical or emotional problem such as chemical abuse (e.g., Alcoholics Anonymous, Cancer Anonymous), loneliness (e.g., Parents Without Partners), AIDS (e.g., ACT-UP), and concerns about relatives (e.g., Al-Anon, Parent-Teacher Associations). Many people with personally experienced problems have the capacity to join with one another to provide mutual support and guidance. These kinds of groups are most likely to endure over time. But it is important to stress that these kinds of self-help groups most likely attract a select population, one that has the capacity to share modest resources with others. Others who have these problems lack that capacity, so help must be provided by the community.

Other kinds of self-help groups do not deal with personally experienced problems. A block association, a good-government league, and a citizens' cleanup association, for example, do not necessarily yield benefits directly and personally to participants. For some members, the satisfaction of participating in these kinds of groups may lie in altruism—"doing good"; others may enjoy a sense of power and control from their participation in these community activities. Generally, these groups do not endure over time without institutional support. Social groups—cliques, gangs, and clubs—in which membership is based on mutual attraction (sometimes called "primary groups") last only as long as the original members remain available to participate.

The relationship between social workers and self-help groups can vary considerably. At one extreme, groups remain entirely autonomous, with the professional serving only to refer people to the group and providing the group with information about social services. At the other extreme (for example, the laryngectomy and mastectomy groups sponsored by some affiliates of the American Cancer Society), the professional takes the major initiative in forming the group, meeting with members on a scheduled basis, and providing resources to the group. There are modified arrangements in between these two extremes.[29]

Various kinds of groups and voluntary associations constitute the method of choice for social work. Evidence for the effectiveness of group interventions for dealing with human problems has been accumulating since the 1930s yet has been largely ignored by social workers. Social psychology provides an extremely rich body of theory for dealing with social problems, but it is not especially useful for psychotherapy.

The acid test of the effectiveness of any social intervention is not whether people "like" the intervention or the professional who provides it. Nor should the test of effectiveness be whether the clients or patients feel better about themselves or have increased self-esteem.[30] The true test of the effectiveness of a social intervention is the degree to which it increases participants' capacities to fulfill their social roles and carry out important social functions relevant to their social status, such as being a student, working, and developing a family. The best test of this capacity is the extent to which it is evident in the groups in which the individual participates in everyday life: at school, on the job, and in the family. Social work that builds a wide variety of the social structures that constitute a community—neighborhood associations, play groups, parents' groups, self-help groups, and so forth—is a more direct way of building the community's capacities to help its members.

Many readers will recall some examples of the great power that social movements, cults, and other kinds of group associations can exert over people's behavior. The most chilling is the Jonestown group in Guyana, led by Reverend Jim Jones, originally of People's Temple in San Francisco. Several hundred families were persuaded to move to Guyana with Jones. Ultimately, most of them died in a mass suicide in 1978. The recent similar experience with the Branch Davidians, in Waco, Texas, is another tragic example.

Any community organization, political group, or religious sect can fall under the control of authoritarian and totalitarian leadership, with tragic results. For that reason, it is exceedingly important that when we consider development of a community-based system of social care in the next chapter, we attend to questions of leadership, governance, and public accountability.

SOCIAL WORK EDUCATION

Standards for social work education in the United States are set by the Council on Social Work Education (CSWE), one of dozens of accrediting bodies established to oversee the education of professionals. The CSWE standards are rather undemanding on the content side. Moreover, there is no hint in them that the accredited schools are for students with a call to serve the poor and needy or to build healthy communities. For example, a 1991 version of the council's revision of its educational policy statement, which leaned heavily in the direction of supporting clinical (psychotherapeutic) social work, made no mention of the importance of serving the poor and deprived, or dependent children, or the mentally ill, or the frail aged.[31] (This oversight was corrected in a later draft after complaints from some members of CSWE.)

In contrast to its flabby educational standards, the council is firm and direct in pushing forward the interests of its most politically demanding members: currently, women, gays, lesbians, and clinical social workers. There are very strong statements in its accreditation standards and its new educational policy statement about the importance of educational institutions employing these groups. As one of our colleagues has pointed out, the council uses "a rubber ruler" to measure schools against standards for hiring personnel from "oppressed" groups. No matter how positive a school's report of its achievements in adding members of these populations to its student body and its faculty, the evaluators can stretch a rubber ruler to any length and say, "Not good enough!"

CSWE's standards for accreditation stipulate that schools must have required classroom courses in the content areas of social policy and programs, methods of practice, human growth and development in the social environment, and research. In addition, there is a requirement for a practicum of at least 900 hours in which the students practice in the field. As a result of the political clout within the profession of racial minorities, lesbians, gays, women, and clinical social workers, there are requirements that there be sufficient content about these groups. There are no requirements for any content about the poor and deprived, or dependent children, or the mentally ill, or the frail aged. Nor is there any requirement that students complete courses on the family, the publicly supported social services, community work, work with groups, or the law. Thus, CSWE leaves rather large gaps in the education of professional social workers.

These deficiencies of social work education reflect the general direction of the field. For the most part, social work educators have failed to provide leadership for the profession. As social work has drifted into the field of psychotherapy, most schools of social work have drifted along with it. Some schools have actively pushed the profession further along in that direction. For example, one dean of a major school of social work is president of his state's association of private psychotherapists. Although they would not announce it publicly, some major schools of social work are known to graduate only professionals who are intending to develop a private practice in psychotherapy.

Recently, the deans and directors of the ten graduate programs in California and the directors of the fifty-eight county social services departments have taken steps to change the direction of social work education in their state. Working with the California chapter of the National Association of Social Workers and with financial support from the Ford Foundation and seven California foundations, they have established the California Social Work Education Center (CalSWEC) at the University of California at Berkeley. It is the objective of CalSWEC to have the majority of social work graduate students in California do their fieldwork in public social service agencies. These students will receive paid fellowships, in exchange for which they must make a commitment to work a year in the public services for each year of fellowship support. The social workers and educators who are involved in CalSWEC have developed a new educational program that prepares professionals for work in the public services. This program provides them with the kinds of knowledge of family law, practical supports, and community services and programs that are needed by professionals in this kind of work. CalSWEC is an innovative and bold program. If it is successful, it may establish a significant new pattern for professional social work in the United States.

But, overall, the majority of social work scholars and educators have little interest in altering the direction of the profession in any significant way. The large majority of teachers in graduate social work education have developed their careers around clinical work and are deeply committed to psychotherapeutic modes of practice. Social work educators, like any other professional educators, tend to be responsive to the interests of their colleagues in the field, in professional associations, and in social service agencies, and they tend to be responsive, too, to the interests of their alumni and the interests of prospective students. As we have noted, larger and larger proportions of the latter enroll in graduate schools of social work with the expectation that their education will prepare them for practicing psychotherapy privately.

If any sort of change is to occur in the ways in which the social work profession serves the community, the impetus for it will have to come primarily from outside social work education. Policymakers and political leaders can have an effect on how professions make use of social resources. If they are dissatisfied, they can cause the profession to behave otherwise by withholding public resources used to pay for professional services and for professional education, or they can provide fiscal and policy incentives to encourage development of a more useful form of social work education and practice.

CHAPTER SEVEN

A PROPOSAL FOR A COMMUNITY-BASED SYSTEM OF SOCIAL CARE

A community-based system of social care will be *universal*— that is, available to everyone; *comprehensive*—providing on one site, all of the kinds of social services required by an urban community; *accessible*—easily reached by all people in the area designated as the service area; and *accountable*—with community residents having a prominent role in making policy for the service and overseeing its implementation.[1] Social services organized in this way have been referred to by different names;[2] we will designate them *community service centers.*

The mode of service delivery we propose is something like what our Victorian ancestors had in mind when they created the settlement house—it is locality based, and it utilizes adult education, social groups, and community associations as its major modes of intervention—but it differs in several ways too: it is publicly financed (with additional support from the voluntary sector); it is not for the poor alone but for all members of the community; and the leadership is not based on social class differences, with middle-class professionals helping lower-class clients, but rather comes from the community it serves.

Over the course of this century, people have become less and less tied to their immediate neighborhood, yet the geographic neighborood continues to be significant for the vast majority of young children and their caretakers and also for the aged. A federal initiative to build community-based systems of social care would be a major step forward in developing family policy in the United States.

A good example of a local initiative for supporting development of community-based services is provided by the Center for Integrated Services for Families and Neighborhoods (CISFAN) in California, established by the deans of the School of Public Health and the School of Social Welfare at the University of California at Berkeley as a means of promoting comprehensive and integrated systems of services for neighborhoods. The center assists local communities to deal with the complex legal, political, financial, and technical problems of establishing these kinds of systems of service.

There are bases other than the neighborhood on which to reorganize social services. The workplace would be a significant alternative. However, large social class differences exist from one workplace to another, and this is an undesirable feature. Moreover, workplace organization would deemphasize concern for children and the family, and it would exclude the aged and unemployed. For these reasons it does not seem to be a desirable means by which to provide services.

A program of social services for a modern community must break dramatically with traditional patterns—with psychotherapeutically oriented approaches to individuals—for providing services. High-quality social services can contribute significantly to enriching all of our lives, and can help to bring Americans together through the experience of mutual caring. This requires that we put behind us some of the mistaken ideas and lingering prejudices about social services that arise from the dustbin of our Victorian past: that social services are only for the poor and disreputable; that social services should achieve their objectives by eradicating individual weaknesses; that social services should be provided to people in the most unattractive way possible lest people should like them; and that social services should be controlled by politicians and professional administrators, our modern-day counterparts of overseers of the poor.

DISCARDING OUTDATED IDEAS

Targeting the Social Services

In a modern community, social services are offered to everyone, not only the poor. There was a time in our not-too-distant past when universal public school education, playgrounds, and public health measures were considered to be radical ideas, and these programs were only for poor people. Better-off people purchased these services on their own. But over time, it was discovered that these services were good for the entire community. Public school education in the twentieth century has served as the major institution for integrating the great masses of immigrants into American society, providing opportunities for upward social mobility never before known, and as an enormous force for democratizing the American community.

The effort to create a universally offered system of social care will encounter in some communities strains that are similar to those of integrating neighborhood schools by busing. However, one of the benefits of a community-based social service system of the kind we are recommending is that it brings together all of the families of the community—children and adults—to work out problems and to share meaningful social and cultural experiences. It is a common saying among policy analysts that programs for poor people usually turn out to be poor programs. A great deal of experience in the public policy field indicates that universal programs tend to be better programs because they serve a cross-section of the total population. Policymakers cannot afford to allow universal programs to be shoddy, or they might suffer politically. This has been the experience with the well-run and highly esteemed social security program, which has strong political support, in contrast to the punitive and stigmatizing Aid to Families with Dependent Children and general assistance programs, the public assistance programs for poor children and mostly single and young parents and unemployed adults, which have poor political support.

Therefore, the center will provide programs to meet the normative needs of all community residents: for example, for child care and for advice, assistance, and guidance with respect to child rearing, health, and family care. There is a simple but not insignificant difference in this way of meeting needs by comparison to more traditional methods of intervention. Instead of being considered "a case" (as in social casework), or "a patient" or "a client" (as in psychotherapy), users of center services will be considered "members," or "service users," or "residents."

Dealing with Social Problems

In order to provide a community-based system of social care, we must break with our psycho-Freudian Victorian pasts. Our Victorian ancestors blamed poverty and other social needs on the evils of sloth and indolence. Many people continue to think in this way about poor people. Today, though, middle-class people are more likely to blame their own problems on the unconscious libidinal evils of unresolved sexual longings, or poor self- esteem, or lack of assertiveness. Both the Victorian and psycho- Freudian ways of thinking are highly individualistic because both locate the cause of problems in the individual and look for solutions in the individual.

In a modern system of community-based social care, we begin with the assumption that the community itself has the capacity to deal with most individually experienced problems through classes, self-help groups, social clubs, recreation groups, special interest groups, and community service organizations. Moreover, we assume that working with community groups is the preferred way to meet social needs because, in addition to solving the individual's problems, we increase the community's overall problem-solving capacity.

Let us say that we want to assist unmarried teenage parents who are reported for child abuse or child neglect. The first step would be to develop a class or a social group for teaching child-rearing skills to these young parents. In the process of learning parenting skills, there will be discussion of the kinds of problems they have been experiencing in raising their children. The primary emphasis will be on the teaching of skills rather than on "treating" the presumed underlying pathology that led to the abuse and neglect. Current social work theory encourages an underestimation of capacity and exaggerates incapacity. It relies heavily on "the myth of intimacy"—the relationship between the professional and the client—and thereby reduces attention to environmental causes of stress and communal sources of strength.[3]

In emphasizing the utilization of communal forms of help, we develop the strengths of the participants rather than weakening them by making them dependent on the approval and support of an individual therapist or caseworker. Also, in the process, the social worker is attentive to the dynamics of the group, encouraging the members to share their experiences, searching for leaders among the members, helping the members form supportive relationships with one another, and helping them to articulate their ideas about what they might want to do as a group. Some members might go on from this experience to make use of other programs offered by, and to provide leadership for, the community service center.

Priorities in Service Provision

The first order of priority in the establishment of center programs should be the development of child care and parent education related to child care—both preschool and after-school care. We select these as the first priorities because they will go a long way in offsetting the possibility of the center's program being perceived as a "welfare" program primarily for poor and troubled people.

Once these programs are well established, others will be added, with priorities established by community leaders with an eye toward building strong political and social support for the community service center. We suggest that the second order of priority should be services for older adults, a service bureau, and a citizens' advice and education bureau, each of which will add additional constituencies that are likely to build broad political support for the center.

The program for older adults will be among the easiest to develop because many communities have run such programs for many years and there are many models from which to build. When possible, the program for older adults should serve as a source of personnel for the child care program.

The service bureau will have the task of recruiting volunteers to assist in and to develop and operate center programs. It will thus be the major source for developing new leadership, a vital need because of the dearth of volunteers resulting from the large numbers of women now in paid employment, who in the past would have been volunteers.

Service in the community service center will be somewhat different from most traditional volunteerism. It will be closer to home; those who give service at the center will be engaging in work that concerns the welfare of their children, friends, neighbors, and others who live in the area. This idea of community service is essential to the center. Service to others is the means by which many people can grow and mature. Certainly, greater provision needs to be made in modern society for "the expression of altruism in the daily life of all social groups."[4]

Those who give service to the center should be honored in annual ceremonies. Currently, volunteer service appears to be assigned primarily as a punishment or a means of recompense for convicted felons. It seems to us to constitute a terrible lesson to the community to encourage this kind of practice. Community service should not be used as a means to punish criminals. The opportunity to give service to the community should be treated as a great honor, reserved for our most outstanding citizens; they should be recognized accordingly.

A second function of the service bureau will be to conduct (with center members) periodic surveys of community needs and resources, to be used in annual program planning by the center's board of directors. Yet another function will be membership recruitment, welcoming people to the center, and orienting them to the center's programs.

The citizens' advice and education bureau, introduced somewhat later in the planning so that there does not develop a perception among either the staff or the program users that counseling and therapy-type activities are central to the center's purpose, will develop an ongoing program of community education about services, programs, and benefits available to citizens in the community at a local, state, and regional and national level. This would occur through a continuing series of public meetings and events, and center publications.

A second function would be to counsel and advise members who need help in selecting center programs for themselves and family members, making referrals of members who have problems for which help is not available in the center, and working with members who are experiencing problems in one of the center programs.

The third function would be taken from the programs of child welfare and adult protective services—foster care, adoptions, and child abuse prevention—that are currently housed in county social services departments. In shifting these programs from social services departments to the center, a new emphasis would be given to utilizing classes and group instruction as the preferred means of providing these services. The citizens' advice and education bureau would seek the highest degree of integration possible with the center's programs of child care and adult eduction.

Protective and surveillance functions with respect to children and dependent adults, however, should be kept in the court and correctional systems and out of the community service center. The argument for separating social control functions from social care functions has been made forcefully by Leroy H. Pelton. The social service agency should have the job of attempting to preserve families, and the police and the courts should be concerned with investigation, prosecution, and enforcement.[5]

The citizens' advice and education bureau would offer the most individualized of the services provided by the community service center. Nonetheless, group and educational modes of service should be the preferred means even with these services. As a policy, the center should provide no individualized services of a psychiatric or psychotherapeutic nature. People seeking these kinds of services or who appear to need them can be referred elsewhere.

A third order of priority in development of center programs should be the establishment of self-help groups (e.g., Alcoholics Anonymous and Parents Without Partners), adult education classes (e.g., painting and money management), a program of physical education, and programs for older teenagers (those sixteen years and over). We have placed this category last because the programs envisioned require that the adult members of the center have a sufficient degree of planning and decision-making capacity to develop these sorts of activities. Were they introduced before there has been sufficient leadership development, the center would have to rely too much on its professional staff for program planning and decision making.

We have not mentioned political action groups, civil rights groups, and social movement kinds of organizations such as the National Organization for Women, National Association for the Advancement of Colored People, and gay and lesbian rights organizations. The provision of public facilities for these kinds of action groups, especially radical and confrontational ones, can cause great political problems for an organization like the center. But once there has been sufficient development of organizational leadership, it can create a good deal of interest and excitement in the community for the center's leadership to consider including organizations of this kind in the center's program. We would advise, though, that these kinds of groups not be considered in the first years of development of the centers.

Social Services Delivery

The community service center should have a mix of some qualities of a public school, a settlement house, an adult education center, and a community center. Its atmosphere will be friendly, relaxed, and stimulating. Indeed, it will be so attractive that people will want to go to the center because they expect that they will meet their friends there and will look forward to engaging in interesting and stimulating activities.

Ideally, it would be best to locate the community service center on the same site as the local elementary school to ensure that the population served by the center is not too large and that the center is geographically accessible. Moreover, elementary school areas constitute a natural community for families with young children, so this location will give a large degree of communality to the center. In addition, there is a high degree of efficiency in this locational arrangement, because the same facility can be used in the daytime for school and child care and in the evening for activities for teenagers and adults. Although we suggest co-location of the community service center and the school, the center should function as an independent community agency.

Both the physical facility and the program should be designed to attract people so that they will keep attending, in the same way that we want people to keep using the public library. Facilities must be spacious, well lighted, and attractively decorated. There must be facilities for recreation and play such as a gym, swimming pool, and games room; facilities for eduction such as classrooms, studios, and a theater with a stage; and facilities for advising and counseling, such as meeting rooms and conference rooms to accommodate groups of all sizes. Finally, the center should have a facility for serving refreshments that is a cross between a British pub and an American soda fountain—a well-appointed, well-run, warm, and welcoming place. A facility of this kind that is inviting and attractive can serve as the social hub of the community.

Providing facilities of high quality will require a shift in the thinking of local political leaders. Currently, most social services departments in the United States are located in unattractive, uncomfortable, and generally unpleasant facilities. Some of them are in dangerous locations.

Leadership

A community-based system of social care is a system for everyone in the community; it is intended to build communality, not to emphasize differences. Our communities need a system of social care that will bring people together to work cooperatively on shared interests: concern for children, neighborhood safety, the quality of public services, and opportunities to share cultural and social values held in common.

To build a system of social care that is truly community based requires that higher levels of government act to promote the capacities of local systems of government to carry these responsibilities. With respect to social care systems, American government can utilize the concept of "subsidiarity" as it is used in the Netherlands; that is, higher levels of government do for lower levels only what they cannot do for themselves.[6]

Social service involves exchange of resources that are highly symbolic and personalistic: support, advocacy, affection, trust, empathy, and self-sufficiency and interventions such as child care, home help, and child abuse prevention. These features suggest that policy decisions about social service programs must be supported on the basis of humanistic, communalistic, and social nurturance values. In recent decades, there has been a considerable diminution in social work of commitment to these values— perhaps because more and more social workers are practicing psychotherapy with middle-class clients who do not need the kinds of protection and advocacy that poor and vulnerable people require, because social workers have been cowed by the tough-minded social policy analysts, and because of the influence on social workers of consumerism and mass culture. It may also have occurred because of insufficient involvement of strong local leadership in development of the social services. To remedy that deficiency requires that professionals concerned about the social services devote considerable energy to cultivating communal leadership and support for these services.

There are three sources from which leadership for the center should be drawn: area residents, representatives of larger units of government, and representatives of voluntary organizations. If the center is to implement the objective of establishing a sense of communality in the area, then policy control for center programs must rest, in large part, with the residents. The establishment of communality requires that people perceive of themselves as being a part of the area and that they believe they share responsibility with others for it. In order to be truly responsible for the center, the residents must have a share of the authority for making decisions about the program and for overseeing how the program is implemented.

In modern urban communities, neighborhoods and other catchment areas can exist comfortably and function efficiently only if there is good coordination of effort with other units of city, county, and state government. Major services of neighborhoods, such as the departments of sanitation, schools, police, recreation, and fire, are maintained by districts, cities, or counties. Public health and welfare are usually operated by counties, but in some states they are run by the state. Schools and parks are usually run by independent districts. Ultimately, the political and financial arrangements for the center itself would probably work most effectively as an independent district with its own taxing power.

Initial financing of the community service center will have to be provided by one or more of these other governmental units, and possibly by a consortium of them. Therefore, it would make sense that these units of government be included in the governance of the center. From the point of view of developing leadership in the center, it should be an important objective to bring about as high an integration as possible of leadership drawn from community service center members and the political leadership in these larger governmental units.

Finally, there are leaders associated with the voluntary sector—organizations like United Way, unions, the NAACP, and the Urban League—whose support and guidance will be useful to the center.

The governing board of the center should contain representatives from each of these sources of community leadership. A temporary board of directors, appointed for approximately two or three years by the mayor and city council, would allow sufficient time to draw up by-laws, plan for the first program priorities, and plan for an election of a board of directors.

The board of directors should be responsible for recruiting and hiring the executive director of the center, who in turn will be responsible for recruiting and selecting a professional staff to work with community leaders to implement the programs of the center. The numbers of staff members will depend upon the number of programs and their size.

ISSUES AND PROBLEMS

Political and Financial Costs

Implementation of the program we propose requires federal and state administrations that can give the political and moral leadership needed to foster communality. The program demands the investment of social and financial resources over time to build the capacity of communities to provide integrated systems of community-based social care.

The financial costs of the proposed program will not be astronomic because public money is already being spent on some parts of it. However, the community service center will provide many new services, and that will increase costs. One might argue that at some time in the future, community-based social care will result in decreased costs of social programs because the center will be more effective than current programs in preventing and ameliorating social problems. However, that is a promise that is made for many new social programs that is hardly ever realized; moreover, the justification of social care cannot be based solely on concerns for economies. We should provide child care services because that will produce healthier and happier children and families. Perhaps it can be argued that good child care programs today will result in savings of money in some tomorrow. However, that politically appealing argument is too complex a proposition to prove; community demands and expectations for services change continuously, new social problems arise continuously, and the technologies and methods for providing care are revised continuously.

It may not be possible to implement the proposed program in its entirety at a time of governmental budget deficits. However, we should take some steps now to begin to reform the system for social service provision using the order of priorities we discussed above. For example, until there is an upturn in employment and an increase in government revenues, efforts to create community service centers should be directed at the poorest communities in the country, with the expectation that the effort will be expanded to all communities when the economy improves. In addition, initial efforts to establish community service centers should be limited to programs for children and the aged, and then expanded to other groups as additional resources become available.

A Never-Ending Romance: Social Work and Psychotherapy

Social work practice has undergone major reformation several times in its relatively short history, but invariably when the crisis ends, the interests of social workers return to psychotherapeutic modes of work.

Efforts to reform social work appear invariably to fail because they are based on the assumption that social work can maintain the great duality with which it has struggled for decades: clinical practice versus social reform. We believe that these two objectives are irreconcilable.

It appears that throughout this century social work has been evolving toward a manifest destiny. Starting as the Cinderella of professions, left for years by psychiatry and psychoanalysis to do society's dirty work of tending to the poor and destitute, social work has finally been transformed into a princess. Sparklingly attired by her fairy godfather, Carl Rogers, she is off to dance at the psychotherapeutic ball with all of the other fifty-minute-hour professionals. Neither wars, nor depressions, nor massive social upheavals have stayed her from her course. And there remain strong forces in the profession that will put up fierce opposition to the course of action we propose: conservative and radical political groups, the social work psychotherapists, and professional social work associations.

Opposition from the Left and Right.   Opposition to our proposals for reform of social services and of social work will face opposition from both the Left and the Right. From the point of view of how best to serve their own interests, conservatives tend to oppose programs that encourage the formation of community groups and organizations. There is a sense that such groups and organizations will necessarily work in opposition to the political establishment.

Experience with the War on Poverty program in the 1960s provides evidence that this is a possibility. The Community Action Programs (CAPs) established in hundreds of local communities to implement the antipoverty programs of the Economic Opportunity Act of 1964 were frequently antiestablishment and confrontational, and they often employed conflict tactics.[7] However, the War on Poverty was in many respects an exceptional situation. First, the legislation was passed in response to the crises brought about by the civil rights revolution that began in the early 1960s. The Economic Opportunity Act of 1964 was an initiative of the Johnson administration aimed primarily at winning the political support of, and providing a new structure of programs for, the great masses of minority poor in urban areas. These were communities in which there were already high degrees of political conflict and social turmoil and low degrees of political and social integration between community residents and the leadership of larger political units.

The War on Poverty program was antiorganizational; the Johnson administration had intentionally bypassed established government in designing the political and organizational framework for the CAPs. The legislation stated that the programs were to be run with the "maximum feasible participation" of the recipients of the services. This laid the basis for high degrees of racial and social class divisiveness and of political conflict over control of the poverty program throughout its history. Senator Daniel Patrick Moynihan later referred to the War on Poverty as the "maximum feasible misunderstanding," especially because of the extraordinary problems of governance it created.[8]

The features of the War on Poverty that created many political difficulties were by no means without some benefits. It was the intention of the Johnson administration and the Bureau of the Budget to try to shake up the established bureaucracies in order to bring about changes in the structure of services, and the CAPs had some degree of success. They did bring about some changes in the nature of service programs and the political processes by which programs were planned and developed. As a result of the CAPs, there have been higher degrees of citizen participation in the planning of public programs, and large cadres of new leadership, especially from minority groups, were developed by the CAPs.

The kinds of program reforms we are recommending differ considerably from the War on Poverty experience. First, the program is intended to serve the entire community, not just the poor and minorities. Second, it will require from the beginning that leadership for the program be broadly based, including program participants of all races and social classes in the community it serves, along with representatives of larger units of government and of organizations from the voluntary sector. And third, the program does not give communities a blank check and absolutely free choice of the programs that are to be provided. We have outlined specific priorities for services that are to be developed by the community service center.

For the most part, social groups and voluntary associations and organizations tend to have a conservatizing and restraining influence on the behaviors of participants. Social groups can exert upon their members strong pressures to conform to the values of the group. When social groups are formed outside the established community context, such as teenage gangs, they frequently tend to encourage deviant and socially destructive behavior. Groups that originate in an open, positive, friendly environment with community encouragement are likely to adopt the values of the community that supports them. For that reason, it is in the community's best interests to invest heavily in the creation of voluntary social groups, organizations, and associations at all age levels.

American communities have been notoriously stingy and lacking in foresight in their failure to invest resources in the development of social and recreational programs for older teenagers and young adults. Across the United States, citizens are dismayed by the destructiveness of teenage gangs and the problem behaviors of teenagers in general. Yet few communities have made substantial provision for the social and recreational needs of this age group.

The propensities of social work's political Left are, in some respects, similar to those of conservatives: both tend to view the welfare state with skepticism. Social workers on the extreme Left refer to themselves as "radical social workers."[9] They are a small proportion of the profession who have had no significant impact on social welfare policy in recent years. The most prominent American social work radicals are Richard A. Cloward and Frances Fox Piven, who were the intellectual leaders of the welfare rights movement of the 1970s and more recently have spearheaded a social movement, Humanserve, that is concerned primarily with increasing voter registration.[10]

Although the radical social workers recruit some young people from social work, they tend not to have a very high regard for the profession or for professional education. For example, Cloward and Piven have written:

> More than a few students perceive the oppressive and conservative character of what is called professional social work education. . . . The infantilization of students is a fundamental mechanism by which the agents of oppression in the welfare state are created. . . . The agencies have made us into policemen. Resistance is necessary in every social welfare setting.[11]

Nonetheless, radical social workers are highly regarded by the profession. Throughout the profession's history, it has honored radicals and muckrakers such as Jane Addams, Clifford Beers,

Saul Alinsky, Cesar Chavez, Jesse Jackson, and Cloward and Piven. These kinds of social critics represent what social workers believe their profession ought to be about. And as the profession becomes increasingly more clinical, the clinicians cling more and more feverishly to these symbols of social reform with less and less direct knowledge of what social reform is about.

Opposition from Psychotherapists. The opposition of psychotherapists to a community-based system of social care is obvious: in a system of social care of the kind we have described, there is little room for them. While we understand that our proposals strike at the livelihood of psychotherapeutically oriented social workers, we do not believe that this should in any way discredit our views. Later, when we present our recommendations for policymakers, we take account of the problems that these reforms may present for social workers who have only clinical knowledge and skills. We believe that with some retraining and continuing education these social workers can make a significant contribution to a community-based system of social care if they desire to be a part of it.

The Organized Profession. We come now to the professional associations. In a 1990 study, Choi found that approximately one-third of the members of the California chapter of the National Association of Social Workers (NASW) reported themselves to be in private practice; an additional 39 percent in agency-based practice reported that in their work they use psychotherapy as their primary practice mode.[12] It is not surprising, then, that NASW devotes a large part of its resources to representing the interests of social work psychotherapists.[13]

The NASW newsletter and its journal, *Social Work,* reflect this dual concern with psychotherapy and with social welfare by being rather Janus-faced. On one page of the national newsletter—usually the first page—they present an image of social work as concerned about the poor, public services, and the need for social change. The following pages are filled with stories of legislative progress made in winning third-party payments for social workers who do psychotherapy, advertisements for social workers to attend conferences on, for example, "Utilizing Transference in Treating Bulimia and Anemia" or "Ego-Syntonic Perturbations of Oedipal Probes," and articles on the economic and legal aspects of starting a private practice. There is a continuous stream of literature from NASW to instruct members about the finer points of private practice.[14]

Social work psychotherapists, through their own organization, the National Societies of Clinical Social Work, keep pressing NASW to serve their interests, including licensing social workers, which has turned out to be licensing for social workers who practice psychotherapy privately because they must compete in the psychotherapy market with other professionals.

If the private practice of social workers doing psychotherapy (or of any other professionals doing psychotherapy) were entirely private, there would be little cause for concern on the part of the community. However, social workers go beyond private transactions in their practice. Most of their business now comes through third-party payments from insurance companies and publicly supported agencies. Thus, "private" practice is not entirely a private matter. Moreover, the organizations of clinicians are extremely effective at lobbying in their own self-interest. They push continuously to increase the size of third-party payments and to extend the conditions that can be covered by these payments.

And they push, too, to require that social work jobs in public and private agencies require licensing. Since the licenses test primarily for psychotherapeutic knowledge and skill, the licensing requirement for positions in the public services has the effect of psychotherapizing the public services. The psychotherapists defend such developments, saying that the requirement of a clinical license for jobs in the public services ensures that even the poor and oppressed will get their fair share of psychotherapy.[15]

It may not be possible to create a sufficiently strong coalition to overcome all of these forces that oppose change. Our proposal for a community-based system of social care requires the support of a large liberal constituency. Liberalism fell into disrepute in the 1980s; however, there is hope that in the later 1990s, under President Clinton, the country will be helped by a revitalized Democratic administration to understand the need to strengthen community-based programs of social care.

Another recent hopeful development in American society is

the growth of interest in the responsive community movement, the philosophy of which is put forth in a new journal, *Responsive Community: Rights and Responsibilities*. Leadership of the movement comes from centrist political and intellectual thinkers like John W. Gardner, Amitai Etzioni, Robert N. Bellah, Alice S. Rossi, Aldai E. Stevension, and Henry Cisneros. The communitarian interest of the movement is highlighted by the emphasis given to the work *and* in the journal's title. Adherents to the principles of the responsive community believe that commitment to and social responsibility for the commons will heal social ills and strengthen democracy. In the journal's first editorial statement, this proposition was presented as follows:

> To the ACLU, libertarians, and other radical individualists, we say that the rights of individuals must be balanced with responsibilities to the community. Individuals are members of a community; neither their existence nor their liberty can be sustained without community. It is empirically wrong and morally dangerous to view individuals as monads or rights-bearers existing in isolation, or to view the commons as merely an aggregation of individuals. The community, in turn, cannot be sustained unless its members dedicate care, energy, and resources to shared projects and do not allow the commons to be consumed by private pursuits. The community has a moral standing coequal to that of the individual.[16]

The Social Worker's Quest for Autonomy

We have mentioned a number of arguments that are put forth to support social work psychotherapy and private practice: the poor need it as much as anyone else; distributive justice demands that they get it; we all use the same theories so we must all be doing the same thing; psychotherapy provides social workers with well-paying jobs; and social workers can do psychotherapy as well as anyone else. There is one more arrow in the quiver of those who argue for private practice: the "quest for autonomy" argument. Robert C. Barker cites studies that show, *"without exception,* that [the private practitioner's] primary motivation is to be free of bureaucratic constraints."[17] There is no other reason, Barker says, such as money or prestige.

It seems to us, though, that this quest for "greater professional freedom and control" and concern for "being our own bosses . . . and avoiding bureaucratic hassles rather than having to do what some supervisor or lawmaker says we have to do" is, more than any other, the quality that makes private practice antithetical to social work practice.[18] Social workers help people to deal with bureaucratic hassles, with the constraints on services set by supervisors, administrators, and lawmakers, and with the complexities of social relations, bureaucracy, and technology in modern society. Most professionals who opt for private practice remove themselves from the problems, settings, and populations that social work was created to deal with. Psychotherapy practiced privately is not a bad or evil thing to do; it's just not social work.

The Contradiction in Values

Our final issue seems to us to be the linchpin of the argument against psychotherapy as a mode of social work practice: the belief systems that underlie all forms of popular psychotherapy are fundamentally and inherently in conflict with communally based kinds of interventions. Therefore, it is not possible to integrate the practice of individual psychotherapy with the practice of communally based systems of social care. There is an inherent conflict between the altruism that is required to build a community-based system of social care and the amoral individualism of psychotherapy.

Social workers who practice the psychotherapeutic arts with an exclusive focus on the individual are more loath than any of the other psychotherapeutic professionals to acknowledge this conflict, and their reluctance to do so is understandable. The idea that the purpose of social work is "to help the person in his situation" is the foremost and longest-standing tenet of the profession. This was the central idea of Mary Richmond's work at the beginning of the century. There is hardly a journal or a book about social work that does not refer to the person-in-the-situation shibboleth. But Richmond's study-diagnosis-treatment approach was based on a medical model of practice, and "inherent in the model was a focus on individual processes which all but ignored the social context in which they are imbedded . . . which resulted in a greater focus on the person than on the situation."[19]

Acknowledging that it is not possible to practice psychotherapy and at the same time attend to the concerns of the community strikes at the social work identity of the social work psychotherapists. However, Eugene W. Kelly, Jr., has pointed out, "Therapeutic individualism, or the 'therapeutic attitude' is philosophically at odds with social commitment."[20] The psychotherapist is, appropriately, interested primarily in the welfare of his or her client.

The major objective of social work practice is to develop and strengthen communally supported services and to enable participants to make use of social resources available to them. Rather than emphasizing their separateness, the professional's function is to draw people into social groups and community activities.

As a mode of intervention, psychotherapy allows for a lower degree of participation and self-determination by service users than any other, and it offers the lowest degree of professional accountability as well. With respect to self-determination, the client in psychotherapy must acknowledge a high degree of reliance and dependence upon the professional and must accept the professional's way of doing business. Psychotherapists deal with this criticism by saying that clients can "vote with their feet." If they are dissatisfied with the treatment, they can discontinue using it. But this is hardly the equivalent of participation and self-determination. Clients meet psychotherapists at moments in their lives when they are extremely insecure and vulnerable; these are times at which they are unlikely to be able to make an informed judgment about the efficacy of the professional's practice.

And apart from licensing procedures and systems of appeal for malpractice and violations of ethical codes, there is a very low degree of accountability for professionals who do psychotherapy. The work of those who are employed in public or voluntary agencies may be supervised and overseen by a superior in the agency. In private practice, there is no oversight of the professional's practice. Thus, psychotherapy as a practice method is antithetical to the development of high degrees of citizen participation and self-determination.

As Bellah and his associates have pointed out in their analysis of American community life, the predominant American value is toward private self-fulfillment, often via psychotherapy, at the expense of social commitment.[21] We believe that a communally based system of social care is, first and foremost, an instrument of the community that, through its representatives and employees, must maintain control over that system. Psychotherapy is, first and foremost, a mode of intervention to serve individuals, one that draws the individual away from the community. It is not a social mode of intervention. For all of these reasons, it is an unsuitable mode of intervention for social work.

RECOMMENDATIONS

Generally we are of the view that professions are incapable of reforming themselves. Professionals of all kinds—social workers, physicians, and attorneys—have learned to practice in a particular way. Most of them have been practicing with some degree of success for a number of years; they find satisfaction, status, and financial benefits in what they do, and they have little reason to want to be reeducated.

Some professionals are engaged in research to improve upon their profession's technology so that their colleagues will be able to do better whatever it is they currently do. But little of this research is intended to revise the major premises and assumptions upon which the professional's practice is based. Incentives for a profession to accept radical change must come from policymakers and political leaders who represent the public interest.

Our recommendations are directed at the ways in which public funds should be directed to build a community-based system of social care and how public funds should be used to support the education of social workers.

The first recommendation is: *that there be established at the federal level in the Department of Health and Human Services a community social care administration* to carry major responsibility for policy and program development for social work and social services at the national level. The administration will have responsibility for establishing federal guidelines to provide funds to states to establish programs of community-based social care. The community social care administration should be founded on the essential principle of subsidiarity discussed earlier in this chapter.

The community social care administration should have subunits to facilitate the development of the elements of the community-based system of social care we have described. The following are some of the possible subunits:

- A community service center bureau with primary responsibility for developing policies, regulations, and guidelines to support state programs to establish community service centers.
- A child care and parent education bureau that will take over some of the child care functions carried by the Department of Health and Human Services and many other departments.
- A volunteer service bureau that will develop policies and programs to foster local volunteerism and community leadership.
- A bureau of social work practice to determine requirements for colleges and universities to receive federal financial support for programs of social work education to prepare professionals to practice in programs of community-based social care and to develop a model social work licensing law for states that is based on practice in community-based social care programs.
- A bureau of self-help organizations to foster policies and programs to support the development of such organizations.
- A national institute of community-based social care to promote and finance research and knowledge development on community-based social care.

The national institute will deal with many of the theoretical and practice issues that will arise in the development of a national system of community-based social care that we have not dealt with in this book. Evaluation of programs would be a major function of the institute. It will be especially valuable to have evaluations that will provide comparisons of systems in communities of different sizes, in different states, and even in different countries. It will be useful, too, to have additional knowledge about different arrangements for, and means for fostering, citizen participation and volunteerism. Currently, relatively little is known in the policy sciences about ways by which to intermingle informal (e.g., family), formal voluntary (e.g., United Way), and formal public (e.g., social services) systems of care. Social workers will need to have much more refined technologies for work with groups and voluntary associations. And, finally, it is essential that we develop a much more refined body of knowledge about various forms of social care and related factors than we now have.

The second recommendation is: *that there be established at state and county levels government-equivalent units of the federal community social care administration* to implement federal guidelines and policies to develop local programs based on the principle of subsidiarity. The states and counties will set policies with specified time limits for social services departments to phase in programs of community-based social care. It seems reasonable to expect that current programs could be converted to community-based social care over a period of six years. As an incentive, federal and state governments should provide administrative and educational supports to counties equivalent to 5 percent of their budgets for each of the six years to support the conversion. Counties would be free to use these funds for program planning and development, in-service training, recruitment, and continuing education.

If implemented, these policies will provide the institutional structure for a twenty-first-century program of community-based social care. This will enable our society to capitalize on the seminal ideas for community social care that were developed by early twentieth-century thinkers like Mary Richmond and Jane Addams.

We stand now at the end of a century of development of social services, in danger of losing the promise of the quintessentially American idea of social work and the hope for community solidarity that lay in the thinking behind the Charity Organization Societies, the Community Chest, the Social Security Act, and the developing American welfare state. That potential richness for community development may be spent on the kinds of frivolous, self-indulgent, and time-limited approaches to problem solving that are offered to us by the psychotherapy industry.

Time is running out. Americans have been socialized for almost a century to believe that psychiatry, psychoanalysis, and humanistic psychology are the only means for dealing with social problems. We seem to be on the verge of turning most of our resources for solving social problems over to the professions that practice the popular psychotherapies.

In order to give a more sensible direction to the use of community resources, we must differentiate between what psychotherapists do and what a community-based system of social care can do. Professionals who claim to do social work should not be secular priests in the church of individual repair. They should be working to build communities. They should not ask, "Does it feel good for *you?*" They should ask, "Is it good for the *community?*" We must not concentrate our resources on helping individuals increase their self-esteem and realize their potential. We must use our resources to help groups in the community to build a community-based system of social care that leads to the creation of healthy communities. That is how we can help to make people healthy.

NOTES

------◆◆◆◆------

Chapter 1: Social Work and Psychotherapy
in the American Community

1. *Common Ground* 53 (Fall 1987), p. 76.
2. Twentieth Annual Conference announcement, Society for Clinical Social Work, Sacramento, 1989.
3. *Common Ground* 52 (Summer 1987), p. 85.
4. *Open Exchange* 14:1 (January–March 1988), p. 35.
5. Benjamin Mankita, "Clinical Social Work Psychoanalytic Conference Breaks New Ground," *National Federation of Societies for Clinical Social Work, Progress Report* 7:1 (Winter 1989), p. 10.
6. *Open Exchange* 14:1 (January–March 1988), p. 12.
7. Ibid. (July–September 1990), p. 54.
8. M.S.W.s are by no means the most outrageous practitioners of the psychotherapeutic arts. Among those who are licensed, the marriage, family, and child counselors tend to make even more excessive claims than the licensed social workers. Among the unlicensed can be found the channelers, hypnotists, herbalists, massagers, spiritualists, bringers of divine love, and other practitioners of strange and perhaps even dangerous therapies. However, our interest is in social work and its relation to the popular psychotherapies, not in psychotherapy per se.
9. These anecdotes are taken from Riva Specht and Grace J. Craig, *Human Development: A Social Work Perspective*, 2d ed. (Englewood Cliffs, N.J.: Prentice-Hall, 1987), pp. 206, 227, 259.
10. See, for example, Charles Murray, *Losing Ground: American Social Policy, 1950–1980* (New York: Basic Books, 1984).
11. Joseph Veroff, Richard A. Kulka, and Elizabeth Douvan, *Mental Health in America: Patterns of Help-Seeking from 1957 to 1976* (New York: Basic Books, 1970), pp. 70, 131–32. We cite figures from this somewhat dated research because it is the only national study ever done of how Americans utilize mental health services that is based on a national sample and includes a 1976 replication of the original 1957 study.

12. Bernie Zilbergeld, *The Shrinking of America: Myths of Psychological Change* (Boston: Little, Brown, 1983), p. 31.

13. Bureau of the Census, *Statistical Abstract of the United States, 1989* (Washington, D.C.: U.S. Government Printing Office, 1989), p. 355; U.S. House of Representatives, Committee on Ways and Means, *1991 Greenbook* (Washington, D.C.: U.S. Government Printing Office, 1991), p. 4.

14. Bureau of the Census, *Statistical Abstract*, p. 368.

15. Gary R. Vandenboss, Nicholas A. Cummings, and Patrick De-Leon, "A Century of Psychotherapy: Economic and Environmental Influences," in Donald K. Freedheim, ed., *History of Psychotherapy: A Century of Change* (Washington, D.C.: American Psychological Association, 1991).

16. Bureau of the Census, *Statistical Abstract*, p. 387.

17. Jean Marbella, "Mental Ills Widespread, Study Says," *Baltimore Sun*, October 16, 1989, p. 1.

18. Ann Kalman Bixby, "Social Welfare Expenditures, Fiscal 1988," *Social Security Bulletin* 54:5 (May 1991), p. 18.

19. In 1988 the poverty level for a family of four was $12,091. Felicity Barringer, "32 Million Lived in Poverty in '88, a Figure Unchanged," *New York Times*, October 19, 1989, p. 1.

20. Bureau of the Census, *Statistical Abstract*, p. 43; Felicity Barringer, "Changes in U.S. Households: Single Parents Amid Solitude," *New York Times*, June 7, 1991, p. 1.

21. Bureau of the Census, *Statistical Abstract of the United States, 1991* (Washington, D.C.: Government Printing Office, 1991).

22. Bureau of the Census, *Statistical Abstracts, 1989*, p. 5.

23. Ibid., p. 371.

24. Sumner M. Rosen, David Fanshel, and Mary E. Lutz, eds., *Face of the Nation* (Silver Spring, Md.: National Association of Social Workers), p. 8.

25. Bureau of the Census, *Statistical Abstracts, 1989*, p. 54.

26. E. Brooks Holifield, *A History of Pastoral Care in America: From Salvation to Self-Realization* (Nashville: Abingdon Press, 1983).

27. Richard Herink, ed., *The Psychotherapy Handbook: The A to Z Guide to More Than 250 Psychotherapies* (New York: New American Library, 1980).

28. See the following critiques of psychotherapy: Paul Halmos, *The Faith of the Counselors* (New York: Schocken Books, 1966); Perry London, *The Modes and Morals of Psychotherapy*, 2d ed. (New York: Hemisphere Publishing Corporation, 1986); O. Hobart Mowrer, *The Crisis in Psychiatry and Religion* (Princeton, N.J.: D. Van Nostrand Company, 1961); Philip Rieff, *The Triumph of the Therapeutic: Uses of Faith After Freud* (New York: Harper & Row, 1966); William Schofield, *Psychotherapy: The Purchase of Friendship* (Englewood Cliffs, N.J.: Prentice-Hall, 1964).

29. The distinction made here between individuals' strivings for happiness versus societal concerns for helping persons meet normative expectations is drawn from Hans H. Strupp and Suzanne Hadley, "A Tripartite Model of Mental Health and Therapeutic Outcomes," *American Psychologist* 32:2 (March 1977), pp. 187–96.

30. Gerald E. Hogarty, "Social Work Practice Research on Severe Mental Illness: Charting a Future," *Research on Social Work Practice* 1 (January 1991), pp. 5–31.

31. California Assembly bill 3659, approved by governor, September 23, 1986.

32. This point is made clearly in the bill establishing the task force: "Low self-esteem may well have a wide-ranging, negative influence on individual conduct, the costs of which both in human and societal terms are manifested in a number of ways, many of which convert into significant expenditure of state moneys. If so, these costs and the costs to government could be reduced by raising the self-esteem level of our citizenry." Ibid.

33. Robert J. Ringer, *Looking Out for Number One* (New York: Funk & Wagnalls, 1977).

34. Melody Beattie, *Codependent No More: How to Stop Controlling Others and Start Caring for Yourself* (New York: Harper & Row, 1987).

35. Ibid., p. 37.

36. Leo Buscaglia, *Loving Each Other: The Challenge of Human Relationships* (New York: Fawcett Columbine, 1986); Beattie, *Codependent No More*.

37. Arthur Wrobel, ed., *Pseudo-Science and Society in Nineteenth-Century America* (Lexington: University Press of Kentucky, 1987).

38. Donald Meyer, *The Positive Thinkers: Popular Religious Psychology from Mary Baker Eddy to Norman Vincent Peale and Ronald Reagan*, rev. ed. (Middletown, Conn.: Weslayan University Press, 1988); Norman Vincent Peale, *The Power of Positive Thinking* (New York: Prentice-Hall, 1952); Joshua Loth Liebman, *Peace of Mind* (New York: Simon and Schuster, 1946); Dale Carnegie, *How to Win Friends and Influence People* (New York: Simon and Schuster, 1936).

39. Carl R. Rogers, *Client-Centered Therapy* (Boston: Houghton Mifflin, 1951).

40. For the story of Rogers's assault on and victory in the academy, see Carl R. Rogers, "Carl R. Rogers," in Edwin G. Boring and Gardner Lindzey, eds., *History of Psychology in Autobiography* (New York: Appleton-Century-Crofts, 1967), 5:343–83; Carl R. Rogers, "In Retrospect: Forty-Six Years," *American Psychologist* 29:2 (February 1974): 46–69.

41. Zilbergeld, *Shrinking of America;* Rieff, *Triumph of the Therapeutic;* London, *Modes and Morals;* Mowrer, *Crisis;* Schofield, *Psychotherapy.*

42. Robert M. Bellah et al., *Habits of the Heart: Individualism and Commitment in American Life* (New York: Harper & Row, 1985).

43. Alexis de Tocqueville, *Democracy in America,* trans. George Lawrence, ed. J. P. Mayer (New York: Doubleday, Anchor Books, 1969); Robert S. Lynd and Helen Newell Lynd, *Middletown: A Study of Contemporary American Culture* (New York: Harcourt, Brace, 1929), and their *Middletown in Transition: A Study* (New York: Harcourt, Brace, 1937).

44. Bellah, *Habits of the Heart,* p. 113.

45. *Proceedings of the First Conference of Charities and Corrections* (Boston: Press of George H. Ellis, 1874), pp. 148–59.

46. Marian C. Putnam, "Friendly Visiting," in *Proceedings of the Fourteenth Conference of Charities and Corrections* (Boston: Press of George H. Ellis, 1887), pp. 148–59.

47. Jane Addams, "Charity and Social Justice," in *Proceedings of the Thirty-seventh Conference of Charities and Corrections* (Fort Wayne, Ind.: Archer Printing Co., 1910), pp. 1–28.

48. Helen Ross and Adelaide M. Johnson, "The Growing Science of Casework," in Cora Kasius, ed., *Principles and Techniques in Social Casework: Selected Articles, 1940–50* (New York: Family Service Association of America, 1950), p. 53.

49. Robert Waelder, "The Scientific Approach to Casework with Special Emphasis on Psychoanalysis," in Kasius, *Principles,* p. 25.

50. Gordon Hamilton, "The Underlying Philosophy of Social Casework," in Kasius, *Principles,* p. 21.

51. William C. Menninger, *Psychiatry: Its Evolution and Present Status* (Ithaca, N.Y.: Cornell University Press, 1948), p. 33.

52. Robert L. Barker, "Private and Proprietary Services," in Anne Minahan, ed., *Encyclopedia of Social Work,* 18th ed. (Silver Spring, Md.: National Association of Social Workers, 1987), pp. 324–29.

53. Ibid.

54. Mark Courtney, "Psychiatric Social Workers and the Early Days of Private Practice," *Social Service Review* 66 (June 1992), pp. 199–214.

55. J. Peck and C. Plotkin, "Social Caseworkers in Private Practice," *Smith College Studies in Social Work* 21:3 (1951), pp. 190–97; S. Koret, "The Social Worker in Private Practice," *Social Work* 3:3 (1958), pp. 11–17; Margaret Golton, "Private Practice in Social Work," in *Encyclopedia of Social Work* (New York: National Association of Social Workers, 1971), p. 950; "Membership Survey Shows Practice Shifts," *NASW News* 28:10 (November 1983), pp. 6–7. Jae Sung Choi, *Members' Views on the California Licensing System for Social Work Practice* (Sacramento: National Association of Social Workers, 1990).

56. "Private vs. Public: The Controversy Continues," in *Progress Re-*

port 9:1 (July 1991), p. 3 (publication of the National Federation of Societies for Clinical Social Work, Arlington, Va.).

57. Robert L. Barker, "Why Do We Do It? It's Not for the Money—Honestly," *Journal of Independent Social Work* 4:1 (1989), p. 1. Also see Barker's *Social Work in Private Practice* (Silver Spring, Md.: National Association of Social Workers, 1989).

58. Pete Buntman, letter to colleagues (Los Alamitos, Calif.: Mental Health Marketing Strategies, 1991), p. 1.

59. Allen Rubin and Peter Johnson, "Direct Practice Interests of Entering MSW Students," *Journal of Social Work Education* 20:2 (Spring 1984), pp. 5–16.

60. Hans S. Falck, *"Journal of Education for Social Work"* 20:2 (1984), p. 4.

61. Herman Borenzweig, "Agency vs. Private Practice: Similarities and Differences," *Social Work* 26:3 (1981), pp. 239–244; see also Thomas G. McGuire et al., "Vendorship and Social Work in Massachusetts," *Social Service Review* 58:3 (1984), pp. 373–83.

62. Robert J. Teare, "Reclassification and Licensing," in Scott Briar et al., 1983–84 *Supplement to the Encyclopedia of Social Work*, 17th ed. (Silver Spring, Md.: National Association of Social Workers, 1983), pp. 120–27; Peter Pecora and M.J. Austin, "Declassification of Social Service Jobs: Issues and Strategies," *Social Work* 28:6 (November–December 1983), pp. 421–26.

Chapter 2: Psychotherapy

1. Joel Kovel, "Therapy in Late Capitalism," *Telos* 30 (Winter 1976–1977), p. 73.

2. Our thinking owes much to Walter Bromberg, *Man Above Humanity: A History of Psychotherapy* (Philadelphia: J. B. Lippincott Company, 1954); Jan Ehrenwald, *Psychotherapy: Myth and Method* (New York: Grune and Stratton, 1966); Jerome Frank, *Persuasion and Healing: A Comparative Study of Psychotherapy*, rev. ed. (Baltimore: Johns Hopkins University Press, 1973); Philip Cushman, "Psychotherapy to 1992: A Historically Situated Interpretation," in Thomas K. Freedheim, ed., *History of Psychotherapy: A Century of Change* (Washington, D.C.: American Psychological Association, 1991).

3. Bromberg, *Man Above Humanity*, p. 21.

4. Jerome Frank's notion of assumptive systems and the way in which they change over time in a culture provides a helpful model for understanding the evaluation of modes of psychological healing. Frank holds that in order for us to function, we must be able to impose some order and regularity on the myriad experiences we face every day. This order takes the form of implicit assumptions about all human beings (including oneself) and the world.

The gestalt formed by these combined assumptions he refers to as a person's "assumptive world."

5. For a philosophical discussion of the psychological dynamics of faith, see Curt John Ducasse, *A Philosophical Scrutiny of Religion* (New York: Ronald, 1952): "'Faith' then apparently means not only (a) very firm belief, either unsupported or insufficiently supported by evidence; but in addition either (b) that the content of the belief tends to be made true by the very act of believing it firmly; or (c) that the content of the belief is of such a nature that firm belief of it tends to have certain valuable results" (p. 74). It is clear that the benefits of at least some forms of psychotherapy rely on the fact that faith in either the method or its practitioner "tends to have certain valuable results."

6. Ehrenwald, *Psychotherapy*, p. 68.

7. Thomas S. Szasz, *The Manufacture of Madness: A Comparative Study of the Inquisition and the Mental Health Movement* (New York: Harper & Row, 1970), pp. 86–87.

8. Bertrand Russell, *A History of Western Philosophy* (New York: Simon & Schuster, 1945).

9. Ibid., p. 538.

10. Ehrenwald, *Psychotherapy*, p. 12.

11. Robert N. Bellah, Richard Madsen, William M. Sullivan, Ann Swidler, and Steven M. Tipton, *Habits of the Heart: Individualism and Commitment in American Life* (New York: Harper & Row, 1985), p. 120.

12. Bromberg, *Man Above Humanity;* Arthur Wrobel, "Phrenology as Political Science," in Wrobel, ed., *Pseudo-Science and Society in Nineteenth-Century America* (Lexington, Ky.: University Press of Kentucky, 1987).

13. Bromberg, *Man Above Humanity*, p. 121.

14. Wrobel, *Pseudo-Science*.

15. John S. Haller, Jr., *American Medicine in Transition: 1840–1910* (Urbana: University of Illinois Press, 1981); Guy Williams, *The Age of Miracles: Medicine and Surgery in the 19th Century* (London: Constable and Company, 1981).

16. Bromberg, *Man Above Humanity*, p. 126.

17. Ibid.; Donald Meyer, *The Positive Thinkers: Popular Religious Psychology from Mary Baker Eddy to Norman Vincent Peale and Ronald Reagan*, rev. ed. (Middletown, Conn.: Weslayan University Press, 1988).

18. Mark Twain, in Bromberg, *Man Above Humanity*, pp. 134–35.

19. Meyer, *Positive Thinkers*.

20. Norman Vincent Peale, *The Power of Positive Thinking* (New York: Prentice-Hall, 1952): Joshua Loth Liebman, *Peace of Mind* (New York: Simon and Schuster, 1946); Dale Carnegie, *How to Win Friends and Influence People* (New York: Simon and Schuster, 1936).

21. William James, *The Varieties of Religious Experience* (New York: Modern Library ed., 1942); Harry Emerson Fosdick, *Adventurous Religion* (New York: Harper and Bros., 1926), and *On Being a Real Person* (New York: Harper and Bros., 1943); George Beard, *American Nervousness* (New York: G. P. Putnam and Sons, 1881); William Warren Bartley, *Werner Erhard: The Transformation of a Man, the Founding of EST* (New York: C. N. Potter, 1978); Lafayette Ron Hubbard, *Dianetics: The Modern Science of Mental Health: A Handbook of Dianetic Therapy* (New York: Hermitage House, 1950).

22. Ralph Waldo Emerson, "Self-Reliance," in Sculley Bradley et al., eds., *The American Tradition in Literature*, 5th ed. (New York: Random House, 1981).

23. Bellah et al., *Habits of the Heart*, p. 334.

24. Beard, *American Nervousness*; S. Weir Mitchell, "The Evolution of the Rest Treatment," *Nervous and Mental Disorders* 31 (1904), p. 368.

25. Bellah, *Habits of the Heart*, pp. 120–21.

26. Emerson, "Self-Reliance," p. 632.

27. Phillip Rieff, *The Triumph of the Therapeutic* (New York: Harper & Row, 1966), p. 73.

28. Ibid., p. 67.

29. The cowboy and the detective provide examples of somewhat dated American character ideals that reflect our individualistic spirit. It is probably not coincidental that neurasthenia and hysteria were common at the turn of the century among women. The message of expressive individualism was not yet one upon which they could act, but it nonetheless had a powerful pull.

30. Sigmund Freud, *The Ego and the Id*, trans. Joan Riviere, ed. James Strachey (New York: W. W. Norton & Co., 1960); Sigmund Freud, *Inhibitions, Symptoms and Anxiety* trans. Alix Strachey, ed. James Strachey (New York: W. W. Norton & Co., 1959).

31. Heinz Hartmann, *Ego Psychology and the Problem of Adaptation* (New York: International Universities Press, 1958); Jacob A. Arlow and Charles Brenner, *Psychoanalytic Concepts and the Structural Theory* (New York: International Universities Press, 1964); Mark Courtney, "The Emperor or His Clothes: The Lacanian and Ego-Psychological Views of the Ego" (master's thesis, John F. Kennedy University, 1987).

32. Rieff, *Triumph*, pp. 74–76.

33. Ibid., p. 76.

34. Carl G. Jung, *The Archetypes and the Collective Unconscious*, 2d ed. trans. R. F. C. Hull (New York: Princeton University Press, 1969).

35. Joseph Campbell, *The Masks of God: Creative Mythology* (New York: Penguin Books, 1968); James Hillman, *Re-Visioning Psychology* (New York: Harper & Row, 1975).

36. David R. Cole, *Helping: Origins and Developments of the Major Psychotherapies* (Toronto: Butterworth & Co., 1982).

37. See, for example, Abraham Maslow, *Toward a Psychology of Being* (New York: Van Nostrand, 1968) and Maslow, *Motivation and Personality* (New York: Harper & Row, 1970); Carl R. Rogers, *Client-Centered Therapy: Its Current Practice, Implications and Theory* (Boston: Houghton Mifflin, 1951) and Rogers, *On Becoming a Person: A Therapist's View of Psychotherapy* (Boston: Houghton Mifflin, 1961).

38. Rollo May, Ernest Angel, and Henri F. Ellenberger, eds., *Existence: A New Dimension in Psychiatry and Psychology* (New York: Simon & Schuster, 1958); Medard Boss, *Psychoanalysis and Daseinsanalysis*, trans. Ludwig B. Lefebre (New York: Basic Books, 1963); Maslow, *Toward a Psychology of Being*; Henryk Misiak and Virginia Staudt Sexton, *Phenomenological, Existential, and Humanistic Psychologies: A Historical Survey* (New York: Grune & Stratton, 1973).

39. Misiak and Sexton, *Phenomenological, Existential, and Humanistic Psychologies*.

40. J. F. T. Bugental, ed., *Challenges of Humanistic Psychology* (New York: McGraw-Hill, 1967); David E. Berlyne, "Humanistic Psychology as a Protest Movement," in Joseph R. Royce and Leendert P. Mos, eds., *Humanistic Psychology: Concepts and Criticisms* (New York: Plenum Press, 1981).

41. Misiak and Sexton, *Phenomenological, Existential, and Humanistic Psychologies*, p. 115.

42. Ibid., p. 125.

43. Maslow did express some interest in the development of community, although he did not have much practical success in this area. Maslow coined the term *eupsychia* to refer to his notion of ideal, human-oriented communities that he believed could be developed by groups of psychologically healthy, "self-actualizing" individuals. To the extent that the self-actualizing members of the eupsychian communities would be actively engaged in seeking personal fulfillment in their work as well as recreation, Maslow believed that nonauthoritarian, enlightened management practices could be developed for eupsychian businesses. Since, according to Maslow's view, there is nothing inherently incompatible about the needs and aspirations of different people, he also assumed that there was nothing incompatible about the goals of workers and management. For a discussion of Maslow's ideas in this regard, see Maslow, *Toward a Psychology of Being*.

44. Ibid., p. iii.

45. See, e.g., Phillip J. Guerin, Jr., ed., *Family Therapy: Theory and Practice* (New York: Gardner Press, 1976); Phillip J. Guerin, Jr., and David R. Chabot, "Development of Family Systems Theory," in Freedheim, ed., *History of Psychotherapy*, pp. 225–60; R. J. Green,

and J. L. Framo, *Family Therapy: Major Contributions* (New York: International Universities Press, 1981); J. Haley and L. Hoffman, *Techniques of Family Therapy* (New York: Basic Books, 1967); S. Minuchin, *Families and Family Therapy* (Cambridge: Harvard University Press, 1974); V. Satir, *Conjoint Family Therapy*, 3d ed. (Palo Alto: Science and Behavior Books, 1983); P. Watzlawick, J. B. Bavelas, and D. D. Jackson, *Pragmatics of Human Communication: A Study of Interactional Patterns, Pathologies, and Paradoxes* (New York: W. W. Norton, 1967).

46. See Guerin and Chabot, "Development of Family Systems Theory"; Minuchin, *Families and Family Therapy*; Paul Watzlawick, Janet B. Bevelas, and Don D. Jackson, *Pragmatics of Human Communication: A Study of Interactional Patterns, Pathologies, and Paradoxes* (New York: W. W. Norton, 1967).

47. Joseph Veroff, Richard A. Kulka, and Elizabeth Douvan, *Mental Health in America: Patterns of Help-Seeking from 1957 to 1976* (New York: Basic Books, 1970).

48. Daniel Gordman, "Social Workers Vault into a Leading Role in Psychotherapy," *New York Times*, April 30, 1985, pp. C-3,9.

49. Bernie Zilbergeld, *The Shrinking of America: Myths of Psychological Change* (Boston: Little, Brown, 1983), p. 32.

50. U.S. Department of Labor, Bureau of Labor Statistics, *Occupational Outlook Handbook* (Washington, D.C.: U.S. Government Printing Office, 1988).

51. Stanton Peele, *Diseasing of America: Addiction Treatment Out of Control* (Lexington, Mass.: Lexington Books, 1989).

52. Nathan Hurvitz, "The Origins of the Peer Self-Help Psychotherapy Group Movement," *Journal of Applied Behavioral Science* 12:3 (1976), pp. 283–94; Alfred H. Katz and Eugene I. Bender, "Self-Help Groups in Western Society: History and Prospects," *Journal of Applied Behavioral Science* 12:3 (1976), pp. 265–82; Alfred H. Katz and Eugene I. Bender, *The Strength in Us: Self-Help Groups in the Modern World* (New York: Franklin-Watts, 1976), p. 9.

53. See, for example, Terry Allen Kupers, "Feminist Men," *Tikkun* 5:4 (July/August 1990), pp. 35–38.

54. David Rieff, "Recovery, Co-Dependency, and the Art of Blaming Somebody Else," *Harpers Magazine* (October 1991), pp. 55–56.

55. Michael Glenn and Richard Kunnes, *Repression or Revolution: Therapy in the United States Today* (New York: Harper & Row, 1973); Joan A. Sayre, "Radical Therapy: A Research Note on the Use of Ideological Work in Maintaining a Deviant Subculture," *Deviant Behavior* 10:4 (1989), pp. 401–12.

56. See, for example, Jewelle Taylor Gibbs, Larke Nahme Huang, and Associates, *Children of Color: Psychological Interventions with Minority Youth* (San Francisco: Jossey-Bass, 1989); Derald Wing Sue and

David Sue, *Counseling the Culturally Different: Theory and Practice* (New York: John Wiley & Sons, 1990).

57. See, for example, Miriam Greenspan, *A New Approach to Women and Therapy* (New York: McGraw-Hill, 1983).

58. Lester Luborsky et al., *Who Will Benefit From Psychotherapy?: Predicting Therapeutic Outcomes* (New York: Basic Books, 1988); Mary Lee Smith et al., *The Benefits of Psychotherapy* (Baltimore: Johns Hopkins University Press, 1980).

59. Jonathan Weisman, "Though Still a Target of Attacks, Self-Esteem Movement Advances," *Education Week*, March 6, 1991, p. 15.

60. "Self-Esteem: Another Word for Goodness," *Economist*, February 2, 1991, pp. 26–27.

61. John Leo, "The Trouble with Self-Esteem," *U.S. News and World Report*, April 2, 1990, p. 16.

62. John Vasconcellos, Preface to *The Social Importance of Self-Esteem*, ed. A. M. Mecca, N. J. Smelser, and J. Vasconcellos (Berkeley: University of California Press, 1989), pp. xiv–xv.

63. Ibid., p. xv.

64. Ibid., p. xvi.

65. See, e.g., "Jack Canfield's Self-Esteem Seminars Newsletter."

66. Vasconcellos, Preface to *Social Importance of Self-Esteem*, p. xvii.

67. Ibid.

68. C. Wright Mills, *The Sociological Imagination* (New York: Oxford University Press, 1959), p. 8.

69. Ibid., p. 6.

70. Ibid., p. 7.

71. The task force had three charges. Its second charge was to collect knowledge about how self-esteem was developed, damaged, lost, and revitalized. This largely consisted of convening a "brainstorming session" with twenty self-esteem "experts," most of whom were therapists or self-esteem trainers. Finally, the task force was to identify model self-esteem programs, which was accomplished by developing a directory of self-esteem-related programs and resources.

72. Mecca, Smelser, and Vasconcellos, *Social Importance of Self-Esteem.*

73. Neil J. Smelser, "Self-Esteem and Social Problems: An Introduction," in ibid., pp. 15, 17.

74. California Task Force to Promote Self-Esteem and Social Responsibility, *Toward a State of Esteem: The Final Report of the California Task Force to Promote Self-Esteem* (Sacramento, Calif.: Bureau of Publications, California State Department of Education, 1990).

75. Ibid.

76. *Jack Canfield's Self-Esteem Seminars Newsletter* (Fall 1990), p. 2.

77. Teresa Moore, "Humanists Talk Politics in San Francisco," *San Francisco Chronicle*, August 3, 1992, p. A18.

Chapter 3: The Emergence of Social Work as a Profession

1. Ferdinand Tonnies, *Community and Society* trans. and ed. Charles Loomis (New York: Harper Torchbooks, 1963).

2. Nina Toren, *Social Work: The Case of a Semi-Profession* (Beverly Hills, Calif.: Sage Publications, 1972).

3. For a more detailed discussion of development of the profession, see Harry Specht, *New Directions for Social Work Practice* (Englewood Cliffs, N.J.: Prentice Hall, 1988; and James Leiby, *The History of Social Welfare and Social Work in the United States* (New York: Columbia University Press, 1978).

4. S. N. Eisenstadt and L. Roniger, *Patrons, Clients, and Friends: Interpersonal Relations and the Structure of Trust in Society* (Cambridge: Cambridge University Press, 1984).

5. J. Q. Wilson, ed., *City Politics and Public Power* (New York: John Wiley, 1968).

6. U.S. Bureau of the Census, *Statistical Abstracts of the U.S., 1991* (Washington, D.C.: U.S. Government Printing Office, 1991), p. 379.

7. Ad Hoc Committee on Advocacy, "The Social Worker as Advocate: Champion of Social Victims," *Social Work* 14 (April 1969), pp. 16–22.

8. Jack Rothman, "Three Models of Community Organization Practice," in *Social Work Practice, 1968* (New York: Columbia University Press, 1968); and George Brager, Harry Specht, and James Torczyner, *Community Organizing*, 2d ed. (New York: Columbia University Press, 1987).

9. Karl Polyani, *The Great Transformation* (New York: Holt, Rinehart & Winston, 1944), p. 80.

10. Karl de Schweinitz, *England's Road to Social Security* (Cranbury, N.J.: A. S. Barnes, 1943).

11. Ibid.

12. President Franklin Pierce, "Veto Message," *Congressional Globe*, May 3, 1854, p. 1062. A century later, another movement for reform of care of the mentally ill viewed the state mental hospitals as "the shame of the states." Under the leadership of Albert Deutsch, this movement succeeded in persuading President Eisenhower to establish the Commission on Care of the Mentally Ill in 1955. The commission's report led to the Community Mental Health Centers Construction Act of 1963 and provided the basis for the 1960s movement for deinstitutionalization of the mentally ill, which led, in the latter part of this century, to the sharp reduction of mentally ill cared for in state mental hospitals. It also led, in part, to one of the great social problems of the 1980s and 1990s: homelessness. In many communities in the United States a large proportion of the homeless are the released mentally ill. The

promised programs of community mental health that were to replace the state hospitals when they closed or reduced their services never materialized. Thus, deinstitutionalization was, in part,
responsible for the problem of homelessness. Joint Commission
on Mental Illness and Health, *Action for Mental Health* (New York:
Basic Books, 1961); E. Fuller Torrey, *Nowhere to Go: The Tragic Od-
yssey of the Homeless Mentally Ill* (New York: Harper & Row, 1989).

13. Neil Gilbert and Barbara Gilbert, *The Enabling State: Modern Welfare Capitalism in America* (New York: Oxford University Press,
1989).

14. Charles Loring Brace, *The Dangerous Classes of New York* (New
York: Wynkoop and Hollenbeck, 1872), p. ii.

15. Amos G. Warner, *American Charities* (New York: Thomas K.
Crowell & Co., 1894), pp. 139–140, 142.

16. From Will Carleton, "Over the Hill to the Poorhouse," in *Farm Bal-
lads* (New York: Harper and Bros., 1882), pp. 51, 52, 56.

17. The bifurcation of social welfare (income supports financed by public programs and social services sponsored by voluntary/private
agencies) provided the institutional structure for the duality that
has marked social work throughout this century. On the one side
are the public social service and social welfare programs to meet
the needs of the poorest and most deprived people in society.
These programs are continuously enmeshed in the rough and
tumble of politics and resultant fighting over civil rights and welfare rights. On the other side are the clinically and psychotherapeutically oriented services offered in private philanthropic voluntary agencies and, more recently, by soical workers in private
practice.

18. Gordon Hamilton, "Refocusing Family Case Work," in *Proceedings
of the National Conference of Social Work, 1931* (Chicago: University
of Chicago Press, 1931), p. 181.

19. Lester Solamon and Alan Abramson, *The Federal Budget and the
Non-profit Sector* (Washington, D.C.: Brookings Institution Press,
1982).

20. June Axinn and Herman Levin, *Social Welfare: A History of the
American Response* (New York: Harper & Row, 1982).

21. George A. Bellamy, "Recreation and Social Progress: The Settlement," in *Proceedings of the National Conference on Charities and Corrections, 1914* (Fort Wayne, Ind.: Fort Wayne Printing, 1914),
pp. 377–78.

22. Reverend Humphries Gurteen, *Handbook of Charity Organization*,
quoted in Patricia Drew, *A Longer View: The Mary E. Richmond Legacy* (Baltimore: School of Social Work, University of Maryland,
1983), p. 7.

23. Ibid., p. 13. Social workers in public agencies were called "investigators" up through the middle of this century, and the term "visi-

tor" was in use through the 1930s; the device of a central registry for applicants for assistance from voluntary charities was in use past midcentury in many American cities.

24. Marian C. Putnam, "Friendly Visiting," in *Proceedings of the 14th Annual Conference of Charities and Corrections* (Boston: A. Williams and Company, 1887), p. 257.

25. Linda Richard, "The Moral Influence of Trained Nurses in Hospitals," in *Proceedings of the National Conference of Charities and Corrections, 1895* (Boston: George H. Ellis, 1895), p. 257.

26. Drew, *A Longer View.*

27. Ibid.

28. Ibid.; Joanna C. Colcord, *The Long View: Papers and Addresses by Mary E. Richmond* (New York: Russell Sage Foundation, 1930).

29. Mary E. Richmond, "Charitable Cooperation," in *Proceedings of the National Conference on Charities and Corrections, 1901* (Boston: George H. Ellis, 1901), pp. 298–313.

30. See, for example, Howard Goldstein, *Social Work Practice: A Unitary Approach* (Columbia, S.C.: University of South Carolina Press, 1973), for a full explanation of how social work theorists use social systems theory.

31. Mary E. Richmond, *Social Diagnosis* (New York: Russell Sage Foundation, 1917).

32. Ibid., p. 62.

33. William G. Black, Jr., "Social Work in World War I: A Method Lost," *Social Service Review* 65 (1991), pp. 379–402.

34. Ibid., p. 396.

35. Mary Richmond, "Some Next Steps in Social Treatment," in *Proceedings of the National Conference on Social Work, 1920* (Chicago: University of Chicago Press, 1920), p. 254.

36. Ibid., p. 256.

37. John Ehrenreich, *The Altruistic Imagination: A History of Social Work and Social Policy in the United States* (Ithaca: Cornell University Press, 1985), p. 90.

38. Addams has been written about extensively. For example, see Jane Addams, *Twenty Years at Hull House* (New York: Macmillan, 1925); Jane Addams, *The Second Twenty Years at Hull House: September 1909 to September 1929* (New York: Macmillan, 1930); James Weber Linn, *Jane Addams* (New York: Appleton-Century, 1935); and Margaret Tims, *Jane Addams of Hull House* (London: George Allen and Unwin, 1961).

39. Tims, *Jane Addams*, p. 62.

40. Ehrenreich, *Altruistic Imagination*, p. 37.

41. Elizabeth Dilling, *The Red Network: A "Who's" and Handbook of Radicalism for Patriots* (Chicago: the Author, 1934), pp. 51–31.

42. Mary Lynn McCrea Bryan and Allen F. Davis, *One Hundred Years*

at Hull House (Bloomington, Ind.: Indiana University Press, 1959), p. 158.

43. Allen F. Davis, *American Heroine: The Life and Legend of Jane Addams* (New York: Oxford University Press, 1973), pp. 266–267.
44. Charlotte Towle, "Social Work: Cause and Function, 1961," *Social Casework* (July 1961), p. 386.
45. Drew, *A Longer View*, p. 20.

Chapter 4: Social Work, the Siren Call of Psychiatry, and the Growth of the Welfare State

1. Abraham Flexner, "Is Social Work a Profession?" in *Proceedings of the National Conference of Charities and Corrections, 1915* (New York: Columbia University Press), pp. 578–79.
2. William G. Black, Jr., "Social Work in World War I: A Method Lost," *Social Service Review* 65 (September 1991), p. 380.
3. Porter R. Lee, *Social Work as Cause and Function and Other Papers* (New York: Columbia University Press, 1937), p. 6.
4. Porter R. Lee, "Changes in Social Thought and Standards Which Affect the Family," in *Proceedings of the National Conference of Social Work, 1923* (Chicago: University of Chicago Press, 1923), p. 287; Lee, "Personality in Social Work," in *Proceedings of the National Conference of Social Work, 1926* (Chicago: University of Chicago Press, 1926), p. 28.
5. Porter R. Lee, "The Administrative Basis of Public Outdoor Relief," in *Proceedings of the National Conference of Social Work, 1917* (Chicago: Hildman Printing Co., 1917), p. 152.
6. Clifford Whittingham Beers, *A Mind That Found Itself: An Autobiography* (Garden City, N.Y.: Doubleday, 1908).
7. Gerald N. Grob, *The Inner World of American Psychiatry, 1890–1940* (New Brunswick, NJ: Rutgers University Press, 1985), p. 10.
8. Psychiatry was recognized as a medical specialization only in 1934. Ibid., p. 232.
9. Fredrick C. Redlich and Daniel K. Freedman, *The Theory and Practice of Psychiatry* (New York: Basic Books, 1966), p. 36.
10. W. H. McClaine, "Relations Existing Between Defective Character and Dependence," in *Proceedings of the National Conference on Charities and Corrections, 1907* (Indianapolis: Wm. B. Buford, 1907), pp. 347–54; A. W. Gutridge, "Investigation," in *Proceedings of the National Conference on Charities and Corrections, 1905* (n.p.: Press of Fred J. Heer, 1905), pp. 359–62 (italics added).
11. Mary E. Richmond, "The Social Case Worker's Task," in *Proceedings of the National Conference on Social Work, 1917* (Chicago: Hildman Printing Co., 1917), pp. 112–115.
12. E. E. Southard, "The Kingdom of Evils: Advantages of an Orderly Approach in Social Case Analysis," in *Proceedings of the National*

Conference of Social Work, 1918 (Chicago: Rosers and Hall Co., 1918), pp. 336–37.

13. R. Macfie Campbell, "The Minimum of Medical Insight Required by Social Service Workers with Delinquents," *Proceedings of the National Conference of Social Work, 1920* (Chicago: University of Chicago Press, 1920), p. 68.

14. Mary Jarrett, "The Psychiatric Thread Running Through All Social Case Work," in *Proceedings of the National Conference of Social Work* (New York: Russell Sage Foundation, 1919).

15. Jessie Taft, "The Social Worker's Opportunity," in *Proceedings of the National Conference of Social Work, 1920* (Chicago, University of Chicago Press, 1920), pp. 374–75 (italics added).

16. See Lois M. French, *Psychiatric Social Work* (New York: Commonwealth Fund, 1940); Marion Kenworthy, "Psychoanalytic Concepts in Mental Hygiene," *Family* 7 (1929), pp. 213–23; Virginia Robinson, *A Changing Psychology in Social Work* (Chapel Hill: University of North Carolina Press, 1930); Jessie Taft, "The Relation of Psychiatry to Social Work," *Family* 7 (1926), pp. 199–203.

17. Clara Bassett, "Psychiatric Social Work," in *The Social Work Yearbook,* ed. Russel Kurz (New York: Russell Sage Foundation, 1939), pp. 312–16; French, *Psychiatric Social Work.*

18. Robinson, *Changing Psychology,* pp. 71–181.

19. Taft, "Relation of Psychiatry," p. 199.

20. Ibid., p. 202.

21. See, Martha H. Field, "Social Casework Practice During the Psychiatric Deluge," *Social Service Review* 54 (1980), pp. 482–507; Stanley Wenocur and Michael Reisch, *From Charity to Enterprise: The Development of American Social Work in a Market Economy* (Chicago: University of Illinois Press, 1989); Robert L. Barker, *Social Work in Private Practice* (Silver Spring, Md.: National Association of Social Workers, 1984).

22. Robinson, *Changing Psychology.*

23. Christine C. Robb, "Changing Goals of Psychiatric Social Work," *News-Letter* 1 (1931), pp. 1–6.

24. Elizabeth Brockett, "Present Practices in Psychiatric Social Work," *News-Letter* 2 (1932), pp. 1–2.

25. French, *Psychiatric Social Work;* Bertha Reynolds, *An Uncharted Journey: Fifty Years of Growth in Social Work* (New York: Citadel Press, 1963).

26. Reynolds, *Uncharted Journey,* pp. 61–62.

27. Ibid., p. 62.

28. Edward D. Lynde, "The Place of Psychiatry in a General Case Work Agency," in *Proceedings of the National Conference of Social Work, 1924* (Chicago: University of Chicago Press, 1924), p. 441.

29. Grace Marcus, "The Status of Social Casework Today," in *Proceedings of the National Conference on Social Work, 1935* (Chicago, Uni-

versity of Chicago Press, 1935), pp. 130, 133, 138. See also *Proceedings of the National Conference of Social Work, 1937,* pp. 385–92; and *Proceedings of the National Conference of Social Work, 1946,* pp. 336–41.

30. Grob, *Inner World,* p. 15.
31. Redlich and Freedman, *Theory and Practice,* p. 9.
32. Mary van Kleeck, "The Common Goals of Labor and Social Work," in *Proceedings of the National Conference on Social Work, 1934* (Chicago: University of Chicago Press, 1934), p. 485.
33. Florence Hollis, "The Functions of a Family Society," *Family* 12 (October 1931), pp. 186–91.
34. Carl R. Rogers, "Carl R. Rogers," in *History of Psychology in Autobiography,* ed. Edwin G. Boring and Gardner Lindzey (New York: Appleton, Century, Crofts, 1967), 5:343–383, and "In Retrospect: Forty-six Years," *American Psychologist* 29 (1974), pp. 46–49.
35. "Moynihan Urges Major Welfare Reform," *Washington Post,* January 22, 1987, p. 1; Jason DeParle, "Fueled by Social Trends, Welfare Cases are Rising," *New York Times,* January 10, 1992, p. 1.
36. Neil Gilbert, *Capitalism and the Welfare State: Dilemmas of Social Benevolence* (New Haven: Yale University Press, 1983).
37. Steven P. Segal and Harry Specht, "A Poorhouse in California, 1983: Oddity or Prelude?" *Social Work* 28 (July–August 1983), pp. 319–22.
38. Neil Gilbert and Harry Specht, *Dimensions of Social Welfare Policy,* 2d ed. (Englewood Cliffs, N.J.: Prentice-Hall, 1986), pp. 161–69.
39. Ibid.
40. *Social Legislation Information Service,* April 23, 1990, pp. 125–26.
41. Marion K. Sanders, "Social Work: A Profession Chasing Its Tail," *Harpers Magazine* 214 (March 1957), pp. 56–62.

Chapter 5: The Movement of Social Work into Private Practice

1. Charlotte S. Henry, "Growing Pains in Psychiatric Social Work," *Journal of Psychiatric Social Work* 27:3 (Winter 1947–1948), p. 90.
2. Jules V. Coleman, "Distinguishing Between Psychotherapy and Casework," *Journal of Social Casework* 30:6 (June 1949), p. 251.
3. David Hardcastle, *The Social Work Labor Force* (Austin: University of Texas at Austin, 1987).
4. Robert L. Barker, *Social Work in Private Practice* (Silver Spring, Md.: National Association of Social Workers, 1984); Sydney Levenstein, *Private Practice in Social Casework* (New York: Columbia University Press, 1964).
5. Mary Richmond, *What Is Social Casework?* (New York: Russell Sage Foundation, 1922), p. 221.
6. See, for example, Howard M. Vollmer and Donald C. Mills, eds., *Professionalization* (Englewood Cliffs, N.J.: Prentice-Hall, 1966).

7. Ernest Greenwood, "Attributes of a Profession," *Social Work* 2:3 (July 1957), pp. 45–55.

8. See Amitai Etzioni, ed., *The Semi-Professions and Their Organization* (New York: Free Press, 1969); Nina Toren, *Social Work: The Case of a Semi-Profession* (Beverly Hills: Sage Publications, 1972).

9. See Terence J. Johnson, *Professions and Power* (London: Macmillan, 1970); Magali Sarfatti Larson, *The Rise of Professionalism* (Berkeley: University of California Press, 1977); Stanley Wenocur and Michael Reisch, "The Social Work Profession and the Ideology of Professionalization," *Journal of Sociology and Social Welfare* 10:4 (November 1973); John H. Ehrenreich, *The Altruistic Imagination: A History of Social Work and Social Policy in the United States* (Ithaca, N.Y.: Cornell University Press, 1985), p. 54.

10. Johnson, *Professions and Power,* p. 45.

11. Barker, *Social Work,* p. 2.

12. American Association of Social Workers, *Compass,* 8:9 (May 1926), pp. 4–5.

13. Lois M. French, *Psychiatric Social Work* (New York: Commonwealth Fund, 1940); Levenstein, *Private Practice.*

14. Francis Taussig, "Widening Horizons in Family Casework," *Family* 6 (1926), pp. 283–86.

15. Ibid., p. 285.

16. Dorothy Kahn, "The Future of Family Social Work," *Family* 9 (1928), p. 185.

17. Ibid., p. 186.

18. Ibid., p. 187.

19. See, e.g., French, *Psychiatric Social Work,* p. 10.

20. Ibid., pp. 10, 101.

21. Levenstein, *Private Practice,* p. 26.

22. See *News-Letter* 1:1 (July 1931), p. 7.

23. Bertha Reynolds, "The Relationship Between Psychiatry and Psychiatric Social Work," *News-Letter* 3:6 (May 1934), pp. 2–3.

24. Barker, *Social Work;* Levenstein, *Private Practice.*

25. Levenstein, *Private Practice.*

26. Lee Rabinowitz Steiner, "Hanging Out a Shingle," *News-Letter* 6:3 (Winter 1936), pp. 1–8.

27. Ibid., p. 1.

28. Ibid.

29. Barker, *Social Work;* Margaret A. Golton, "Private Practice in Social Work," in *Encyclopedia of Social Work,* 16th ed. (New York: National Association of Social Workers, 1971).

30. French, *Psychiatric Social Work;* Bertha Reynolds, *An Uncharted Journey: Fifty Years of Growth in Social Work* (New York: Citadel Press, 1963).

31. French, *Psychiatric Social Work.*

32. See, e.g., Annette Garrett, "Historical Survey of the Evolution of

Casework," *Journal of Social Casework* 30:6 (1949), pp. 219–29; Florence Hollis, "The Techniques of Casework," *Journal of Social Casework* 30:6 (June 1949), pp. 235–44.

33. Garret, "Historical Survey."
34. Hollis, "Techniques," pp. 236, 242.
35. Felix Deutsch, "Condensation of the Discussion," *Journal of Social Casework* 30:6 (June 1949), p. 252.
36. See Martha Dore, "Functional Theory: Its History and Influence on Contemporary Social Work Practice," *Social Service Review* 64:3 (September 1990), pp. 358–74; Virginia Robinson, ed., *Training for Skill in Social Casework* (Philadelphia: University of Pennsylvania Press, 1942); Ruth Smalley, "Psychiatric Social Worker or Psychotherapist?" *Journal of Psychiatric Social Work* 16 (Spring 1947), pp. 107–10; Jessie Taft, "The Relation of Function to Process in Social Casework," *Journal of Social Work Process* 1 (November 1937), pp. 1–18.
37. Smalley, "Psychiatric Social Worker," p. 108.
38. Dore, "Functional Theory."
39. Rowena Ryerson and Elizabeth Weller, "The Private Practice of Psychiatric Casework," *Journal of Psychiatric Social Work* 16 (Spring 1947), pp. 112, 115.
40. Ibid., p. 112.
41. Josephine Peek and Charlotte Plotkin, "Social Caseworkers in Private Practice," *Smith College Studies in Social Work* 21:3 (1951), p. 165.
42. Ibid., pp. 167, 171, 172–75.
43. Ibid., pp. 173–74, 175.
44. Ibid., p. 176.
45. Ibid., pp. 177–78, 182.
46. Ibid., pp. 185, 194.
47. Ibid., pp. 192–95.
48. Golton, "Private Practice," p. 950.
49. Gary R. Vandenboss, Nicholas A. Cummings, and Patrick H. DeLeon, "A Century of Psychotherapy: Economic and Environmental Influences," in Donald K. Freedheim (ed.) *History of Psychotherapy: A Century of Change* (Washington, D.C.: American Psychological Association, 1991), pp. 65–102; Golton, "Private Practice," p. 951.
50. Phil Brown, "Social Workers in Private Practice: What Are They Really Doing," *Clinical Social Work Journal* 18:4 (Winter 1990), pp. 407–21.
51. Larson, *Rise of Professionalism.*
52. David Wagner, "Collective Mobility and Fragmentation: A Model of Social Work History," *Journal of Sociology and Social Welfare* 13:3 (September 1986), pp. 657–700; Stanley Wenocur and Michael Reisch, "The Social Work Profession and the Ideology of Profes-

sionalism," *Journal of Sociology and Social Welfare* 10:4 (November 1983), pp. 684–732.

53. Coleman, "Distinguishing Between Psychotherapy and Casework," pp. 246, 248.

54. Smalley, "Psychiatric Social Worker," p. 109.

55. Hardcastle, *Social Work Labor Force*, p. 23.

56. Srinika Jayaratne, Kristine Siefert, and Wayne A. Chess, "Private and Agency Practitioners: Some Data and Observations," *Social Service Review* 62:2 (June 1988), pp. 325–36.

57. Jae-sung Choi, "Members' Views on the California Licensing System for Social Work Practice," California chapter, National Association of Social Workers, November 29, 1990.

58. Hardcastle, *Social Work Labor Force*, p. 22; Daniel Gordman, "Social Workers Vault into a Leading Role of Psychotherapy," *New York Times*, April 30, 1985, pp. C3, C9.

59. U.S. Department of Labor, Bureau of Labor Statistics, *Occupational Outlook Handbook* (Washington, D.C.: U.S. Government Printing Office, 1989), p. 117.

60. Neil Abell and James R. McDonell, "Preparing for Practice: Motivations, Expectations and Aspirations of the MSW Class of 1990," *Journal of Social Work Education* 26 (1990), pp. 57–64; Amy C. .Butler, "A Reevaluation of Social Work Students' Career Interests," *Journal of Social Work Education* 26 (1990), pp. 44–56; Allen Rubin and Peter J. Johnson, "Direct Practice Interests of Entering MSW Students," *Journal of Social Work Education* 20 (1984), pp. 5–16; Allen Rubin, Peter J. Johnson, and Kevin L. DeWeaver, "Direct Practice Interests of MSW Students: Changes from Entry to Graduation," *Journal of Social Work Education* 22 (1986), pp. 98–108. These surveys asked students what they expect to be doing in five years. Since it appears that most private practitioners enter practice around ten years after completing their M.S.W., this approach may understate the desire to enter private practice.

61. Butler, "Reevaluation"; Rubin and Johnson, "Direct Practice Interests."

62. See Brown, "Social Workers in Private Practice"; Herman Borenzweig, "Agency vs. Private Practice: Similarities and Differences," *Social Work* 26 (1981), pp. 239–44; Michael Cohen, "Some Characteristics of Social Workers in Private Practice," *Social Work* 11 (1966), pp. 69–77; René C. Grosser and Stephen R. Block, "Clinical Social Work Practice in the Private Sector: A Survey," *Clinical Social Work Journal* 11 (1983), pp. 245–62; Jayaratne, Siefert, and Chess, "Private and Agency Practitioners"; Michael Kriegsfeld, "The Private Practice of Social Work," in *The Eighth Annual Conference Proceedings* (Bakersfield, Calif.: Conference for the Advancement of Private Practice in Social Work, 1969); Levenstein, *Private*

Practice; Peek and Plotkin, "Social Caseworkers"; Ryerson and Weller, "Private Practice"; and Marquis Earl Wallace, "Private Practice: A Nationwide Study," *Social Work* 27 (1982), pp. 262–67.

63. See "Some Characteristics"; Levenstein, *Private Practice*; Wallace, "Private Practice"; Jayaratne, Siefert, and Chess, "Private Agency Practitioners."

64. Brown, "Social Workers in Private Practice."

65. See Patricia Ewalt, ed., *Toward a Definition of Clinical Social Work* (Washington, D.C.: National Association of Social Workers, 1979).

66. Jerome C. Wakefield, "Psychotherapy, Distributive Justice, and Social Work. Part 2: Psychotherapy and the Pursuit of Justice," *Social Service Review* 62 (1988), p. 377.

67. Srinika Jayaratne, "A Study of Clinical Eclecticism," *Social Service Review* 52 (1978), pp. 621–31.

68. John Goldmeier, "Private Practice and the Purchase of Services: Who Are the Practitioners?" *American Journal of Orthopsychiatry* 56 (1986), pp. 89–102.

69. Vincent J. Giannetti and Richard A. Wells, "Psychotherapeutic Outcome and Professional Affiliation," *Social Service Review* 59 (March 1985), p. 38.

70. William E. Henry, John H. Sims, and S. Lee Spray, *The Fifth Profession* (San Francisco: Jossey-Bass, 1971).

71. Wallace, "Private Practice," p. 266.

72. In contrast to our position, there are those within the social work profession whose definition of clinical social work practice would include most psychotherapists of any professional background within the ranks of social work. Wakefield's attempt in "Psychotherapy" to provide a philosophical justification for psychotherapeutic practice by social workers is an excellent example of this form of turf redefinition. He argues that psychotherapeutic interventions can function as a form of compensation for earlier deprivation of psychological needs. From this perspective, psychotherapy is seen as a form of restitution and thus serves to provide for distributive justice. Wakefield's suggestion that this position is "highly controversial" within the therapy field seems to imply that social workers are uniquely suited to carrying out this project of redistributive justice and filling a critical void in the psychotherapy market.

Wakefield seems to have missed the fact that there are already thousands of therapists and recovery gurus making a living off the deprived "inner children" of their clients. His view of clinical social work would result in a redefinition of many psychologists, marriage and family counselors, and even psychiatrists as social workers, rather than delineating a unique psychotherapeutic role for social work clinicians.

73. Timothy Lause, "Professional Social Work Associations and Legislative Action: 1974 to 1977," *Journal of Sociology and Social Welfare* 6 (1979), pp. 265–73.
74. Michael Sherraden, "The Business of Social Work," *Encyclopedia of Social Work,* 18th ed., 1990 Supplement (Silver Spring, Md.: National Association of Social Workers, 1990), p. 55.
75. Nicholas A. Cummings, "The Future of Psychotherapy: One Psychologist's Perspective," *American Journal of Psychotherapy* 41:3 (July 1987), pp. 349–60.

Chapter 6: Social Work in the Twenty-first Century

1. C. Wright Mills, *The Sociological Imagination* (New York: Grove Press, 1961), especially the discussion of private troubles and public issues, p. 8.
2. See, for example, Alfred J. Kahn and Sheila Kamerman, *Not for the Poor Alone: European Social Services* (New York: Harper & Row, 1975).
3. Ernest Greenwood, "Attributes of a Profession," *Social Work* 2:3 (1957), pp. 45–55.
4. Robert Pruger and Harry Specht, "Establishing New Careers Programs: Organizational Barriers and Strategies," *Social Work* 4:13 (1968), p. 25.
5. Marie P. Haug and Marvin B. Sussman, "Professional Autonomy and the Revolt of the Client," *Social Problems* 17 (1969), pp. 153–61.
6. Eugene Litwak and Henry J. Meyer, *School, Family, and Neighborhood: The Theory and Practice of Community Relations* (New York: Columbia University Press, 1974).
7. Urie Bronfenbrenner, "The Disturbing Changes in the American Family," *Search* 21 (1976), p. 14.
8. Michael Novak, "The Family Out of Favor," *Harpers* (April 1976), pp. 37–46.
9. William B. Stiles, David A. Shapiro, and Robert Elliott, "Are All Psychotherapies Equivalent?" *American Psychologist* 41 (February 1986), p. 165.
10. Moshe Talmon, *Single-Session Therapy: Maximizing the Effect of the First (and Often Only) Therapeutic Encounter* (San Francisco: Jossey-Bass, 1990); see also Dan Goleman, "When to Challenge the Therapist—and Why," *Psychology Updates* (New York: Harper, Collins Publishers, 1991), pp. 233–35.
11. Bernie Zilbergeld, *The Shrinking of America* (Boston: Little, Brown, 1983).
12. Bonnie Bhatti, David Derezotes, Sun-yuk Kim, and Harry Specht, "The Associations Between Child Maltreatment and Self-Esteem," in Andy Mecca, Neil Smelser, and John Vasconcellos, eds., *The So-*

cial Importance of Self-Esteem (Berkeley: University of California Press, 1989).

13. Paul Saxton, "Comments on Social Work and the Psychotherapies," *Social Service Review* 65 (1991), pp. 315–16.

14. Ibid., p. 316.

15. The following readings in social psychology and sociology are important for social workers: Fred M. Cox, Charles Garvin, John Ehrlich, and Jack Rothman, *Strategies of Community Organization*, 4th ed. (Itasca, Ill.: F. E. Peacock, Publishers, 1987); John W. Thibaut and Harold H. Kelley, *The Social Psychology of Groups* (New York: John Wiley, 1959); Barry Wellman, "Applying Network Analysis is the Study of Social Support," in Benjamin H. Gottlieb, ed., *Social Networks and Social Support* (Beverly Hills, Calif.: Sage Publications, 1981); Harold Weissman, Irwin Epstein, and Andrea Savage, *Agency-Based Social Work* (Philadelphia: Temple University Press, 1983); Peter M. Blau, *Exchange and Power in Social Life* (New York: John Wiley, 1964); Fritz Heider, *The Psychology of Interpersonal Relations* (New York: John Wiley, 1958).

16. Aaron Rosen and Sheila Livne, "Personal versus Environmental Factors in Social Workers' Perceptions of Client Problems," *Social Service Review* 66:1 (1992), pp. 85–96.

17. Guy E. Swanson, "Social Foundations and Personal Development" (University of California at Berkeley, Institute of Human Development, 1976, mimeographed), and "Toward Corporate Action: A Reconstruction of Elementary Collective Processes," in Tomatsu Shibutani, ed., *Human Nature and Collective Behavior: Papers in Honor of Herbert Blumer* (Englewood Cliffs, N.J.: Prentice-Hall, 1970), pp. 29–46.

18. Ibid.

19. C. Wendell King, *Social Movements in the United States* (New York: Random House, 1956); George F. E. Rudé, *The Crowd in History: A Study of Population Disturbances in France and England, 1730–1848* (London: Lawrence and Wishart, 1981); Beulah Rothman and Catherine P. Papell, "Social Group Work Models: Possession and Heritage," *Journal of Education for Social Work* 2:2 (1966), pp. 66–77.

20. Swanson, "Social Foundations."

21. Richard M. Lerner, "A Dynamic Interactional Concept of Individual and Social Relationship Development," in Robert L. Burgess and Ted L. Huston, eds., *Social Exchange in Developing Relationships* (New York: Academic Press, 1979), p. 291.

22. Harriet B. Braiker and Harold H. Kelley, "Conflict in Development of Close Relationships," in Burgess and Huston, *Social Exchange*, pp. 137–40.

23. Eileen Gambrill and Cheryl Richey, *Taking Care of Your Social Life* (Belmont, Calif.: Wadsworth, 1985).

24. S. Starker, *Oracle at the Supermarket* (New Brunswick, N.J.: Trans-

action Books, 1989); Dale Carnegie, *How to Win Friends and Influence People* (New York: Simon and Schuster, 1936); Gambrill and Richey, *Taking Charge.*

25. J. Richard Eiser, *Cognitive Social Psychology: A Guidebook to Theory and Research* (London: McGraw-Hill, 1980), pp. 273–77; and R. C. Ziller, "Four Techniques of Group Decision Under Uncertainty," *Journal of Applied Psychology* 41 (1957), pp. 384–88.

26. S. Muscovici and M. Zavaloni, "The Group as a Polarizer of Attitudes," *Journal of Personality and Social Psychology* 2 (1969), pp. 124–35; N. Kogan and M. A. Wallach, *Risk-taking: A Study in Cognition and Personality* (New York: Holt, Rinehart, and Winston, 1964); and A. I. Teget and D. G. Pruitt, "Components of Risk Taking," *Journal of Experimental Social Psychology* 3 (1967), pp. 189–205.

27. Charlan Jeanne Nemeth, "The Differential Contributions of Majority and Minority Influence," *Psychological Review* 93:1 (1986), pp. 23–32.

28. Kurt Lewin, "Group Decision and Social Change," in T. Newcomb and E. Hartley, eds., *Readings in Social Psychology* (New York: Henry Holt, 1947), pp. 330–344.

29. Robert Adams, *Self-Help, Social Work and Empowerment* (London: Macmillan, 1990), pp. 34–35.

30. In fact, the objective of some social interventions is to increase an individual's anxiety and to lower self-esteem. An example of this is a television spot produced by the National Council on Child Abuse Prevention in which parents are heard making disparaging and threatening remarks to their children. At the end of the commercial a large tear rolls down a child's cheek. This is surely intended to lower the self-esteem and increase the anxiety of abusing parents. It is also a good example of a television behavioral intervention.

31. Commission on Educational Policy and Planning, Council on Social Work Education, "Curriculum Policy Statement for Master's Degree Programs in Social Work Education," third draft (Alexandria, Va.: Council on Social Work Education, February 13, 1992).

Chapter 7: A Proposal for a Community-Based System of Social Care

1. We have taken the term "community-based system of social care" from Wally Harbert and Paul Rogers, eds., *Community-Based Social Care: The Avon Experience* (London: Bedford Square Press, 1983).

2. Gerald Smale et al., *Community Social Work: A Paradigm for Change* (London: National Institute for Social Work, 1988).

3. Malcolm Bush, *Families in Distress* (Berkeley: University of California Press), p. 286.

4. Richard Titmuss, *The Gift Relationship* (New York: Pantheon, 1971), p. 324.

5. Leroy H. Pelton, *For Reasons of Poverty* (New York: Praeger Publishers, 1989).

6. Ralph M. Kramer, *Voluntary Agencies in the Welfare State* (Berkeley: University of California Press, 1981). Kramer describes the principles of subsidiarity as "a welfare ideology based on the Thomistic principle of subsidiarity and the Protestant equivalent, sphere sovereignty. In practice, this has been taken to mean that if an individual citizen or a lower social unit is unable to carry out a desirable objective, then the obligation of higher authority is restricted to providing the necessary financial support. In this conception, government is viewed as a residual, last-resort institution when other, more primary ones are unable to function. Government becomes the financier . . . of a service, on the assumption that the service should stay as close as possible to the person in need. A corollary belief is that government should interfere as little as possible in the work of the more primary social units; 'give us the money, but hands-off' is a crude statement of the operating principle" (pp. 23–24).

7. Daniel P. Moynihan, *Maximum Feasible Misunderstanding* (New York: Free Press, 1969); Ralph M. Kramer, *The Participation of the Poor: Comparative Community Case Studies in the War on Poverty* (Englewood Cliffs, N.J.: Prentice-Hall, 1969).

8. Moynihan, *Maximum Feasible Misunderstanding.*

9. Roy Bailey and Mike Brake, eds., *Radical Social Work* (New York: Pantheon Books, 1976); Ann Withorn, *Serving the People: Social Services and Social Change* (New York: Columbia University Press, 1984).

10. Richard Cloward and Lloyd Ohlin, *Delinquency and Opportunity: A Theory of Delinquent Gangs* (Glencoe, Ill.: Free Press, 1965); Frances Fox Piven and Richard A. Cloward, *Regulating the Poor: The Functions of Public Welfare* (New York: Pantheon Books, 1971).

11. Richard A. Cloward and Frances Fox Piven, "Notes Toward a Radical Social Work," in Bailey and Brake, *Radical Social Work,* pp. vii, xvi, xxii, xxxiv.

12. Jae Sung Choi, *Members' Views of the California Licensing System for Social Work Practice* (Sacramento, Calif., 1990).

13. Michael Sherraden, "The Business of Social Work," in *Encyclopedia of Social Work: 1990 Supplement,* 18th ed. (Silver Spring, Md.: National Association of Social Workers, 1990), p. 55; Mark G. Battle, "National Association of Social Workers," in *Encyclopedia of Social Work,* p. 232; Don Knoll, president, National Institute for Clinical Social Work Advancement, letter, February 27, 1990.

14. For example, see Robert L. Barker, *Social Work and Private Practice*

(Silver Spring, Md.: National Association of Social Workers, 1989).

15. Paul Saxton, "Comments on 'Social Work and the Psychothera-
pies,'" *Social Service Review* 65:2 (1991), pp. 314–17; Jerome C.
Wakefield, "Why Psychotherapeutic Social Work Don't Get No
Re-Specht," *Social Service Review* 66:1 (1992), pp. 141–51.

16. Amitai Etzioni, Jim Fishkin, William Galston, and Mary Ann
Glendon, "Editorial Statement," *Responsive Community: Rights and
Responsibilities* 1:1 (Winter 1990–1991), p. 2.

17. Robert L. Barker, Editorial, "Why Do We Do It? It's Not for the
Money—Honestly!" *Journal of Independent Social Work* 4:1 (1989),
p. 1 (italics added).

18. Ibid.

19. Carel Germain, quoted in Patricia Drew, *A Longer View: The Mary
E. Richmond Legacy* (Baltimore: University of Maryland, School of
Social Work, 1983), p. 51.

20. Eugene W. Kelley, Jr., "Social Commitment and Individual Counseling," *Journal of Counseling and Development* 67 (February 1989),
p. 341.

21. Robert M. Bellah et al., *Habits of the Heart: Individualism and Commitment in American Life* (New York: Harper & Row, 1985), p. 107.

INDEX